GRIFFIN—

You are a great
disappointment to me.

The tales of Georgia Tech's
Dean Emeritus George C. Griffin

Atlanta, Georgia
The Georgia Tech National Alumni Association, Inc.
1971

GRIFF

You are a grea

disappointm

The tales of Geor

Dean Emeritus Geor

Atlanta, Geo

The Georgia Tech National A

1971

To

Eugenia Johnston Griffin

who has put up with me for 47 years

PREFACE

It is believed that the writer was the first man to receive the Heisman Award. I am still waiting for this statement to be disproved.

One day as I was walking west on North Avenue, Coach Heisman was on the other side of the street headed east. All of a sudden the old man shouted "Griffin, I would like to see you a minute." I gladly crossed the street, wondering what Coach wanted, hoping it was a good word for my fine work on the gridiron. Then it came forth. "Griffin, you are a great disappointment to me."

I was finally brave enough to ask "Coach, why am I a great disappointment to you?" "Well," he said, "I always expect you to get away for a long run, but you NEVER DO."

With that he continued his stroll, leaving me with a great weight that I have carried for lo these 54 years.

I want to thank the Alumni of Georgia Tech who have been so kind to me over the years and hope you will enjoy these true (?) stories Alex and I have been telling and retelling since the days of Coach Heisman and Dr. Matheson.

My due appreciation to Ben Moon, Director of Publications; Dick Link, Director of Information Services; Roane Beard, Director of the Georgia Tech National Alumni Association; Joe Guthridge, Vice President for Development; Tom Hall, Director of Resources Development; the late Bob Wallace, Director of Information Services and Publications; Jimmy Ramage, President of the Georgia Tech Alumni Association for 1970-71, who read over the manuscript (his comments about my typing and spelling are not worth repeating); Mrs. Charlotte Darby of the Alumni Association; and Miss Cathy Kramer of the Office of Publications.

Table of Contents

How Griffin Got Here

One day a little lad about 10 years old, living in Savannah, was leafing through a magazine—this was 65 years ago. He saw a picture of a young man, in khakis, with boots on, looking through a strange instrument. The picture was an ad from Georgia Tech telling all about the Civil Engineering Department. Immediately, this lad decided he wanted to go to Georgia Tech and use one of those instruments. Later his family moved to Atlanta where he finished grammar school, went to old Boy's High School for a couple of years and then to Peacock Fleet School, where he managed to get together eight credits so he could enter Georgia Tech.

In those days there were very few four-year high schools in the state, so Tech operated on what was known as the Apprentice Class, better known as the Sub Class or Subs. It was really the fourth year of high school and if you passed everything you were admitted to the Freshman class in college the next fall.

In September of 1914, as a skinny lad of 120 pounds, with a pompadour, I finally realized my youthful ambition and enrolled in this gristmill. (As John Young, the famous astronaut puts it, you just can't say enough for what you receive at Tech.)

Messrs. Hugh Caldwell and Tommy Branch handled the registration and away I went. I happen to remember three of our professors—Mr. Williams, who left to teach in a girl's college after three or four years, Mr. Ferguson from Yale, who taught English and ancient history, and the mighty Professor William A. Alexander. "Fergy" with his guitar and Alex with his great knowledge of math managed to keep us on the straight and narrow. We were the last of the Subs, and I can well remember at the Tech-

Georgia baseball game in Atlanta how the Subs held a parade, all
44 of us, carrying a coffin with pallbearers and all the trimmings
and buried the Subs in the corner of where the West Stands now
exist. It was a rather noisy funeral because some of the fellows
had brought a boiler down to the field; they steamed her up,
attached a whistle and just about ran everyone out of Grant Field.
A great gang. There were some great students in that class. Most
of us passed into the Freshman class, but darn few of us ever
finished. Personally I thought I was a pretty good brain until I
entered the Lyman Hall Building, known as the Chemistry Department. Three times I tried that freshman chemistry before I
could get out of the clutches of Dr. Boggs, Dr. Daniel and others
only to pass into the clutches of Big Doc and Dr. Wroth. What a
life. Physics, where I had to contend with Shortstop Bortell and
Tobe, was just about as bad. Old Bortell really wore me out before
I could get out of that department. The only way I could get even
was to beat him at tennis once in a while. I remember one day
when Mrs. Bortell came by to pick him up, and in his presence
said "please do me a favor; don't beat my husband playing tennis.
He isn't fit to live with for a week."

One of the most interesting parts of life as Subs was the fact
that in those days class athletics were in full swing and, since we
had only 44 men in our class, everyone had a chance to play some
game or another. For instance, in football only eleven men came
out for the team.

Everyone made it and away we went as the season started.
Coach Alex was our coach and was our referee each Saturday.
With his fine coaching and his eagle eye on Saturday we never
lost a game. We always tied and couldn't win one no matter how
hard we tried. As hard luck would have it Dawson Teague, who
played fullback, came down the steps at his fraternity house on
North Avenue, slipped and all of a sudden a good football player
was washed out. Dawson was later on the varsity squad. There
was nothing left for Alex to do but to continue his coaching and
play fullback on Saturdays. Well, we were glad to have him on
the team so we could continue in the league, but he wasn't much

good to us. His work as referee on Saturdays was ten times more valuable. Our first game after the addition of William Anderson Alexander to the team was a great bust. We lost the game 59 to 0. What a sad day. When baseball and basketball rolled around, we managed to get through alive. The same could be said for track.

One of my classmates entered the Marine Corps and was killed in France. He was a lieutenant.

Professor Stamy, who was always talking about the famous problems, was also one of our math professors. He was a great teacher and one of the hardest working men at Tech. Dr. Matheson was· our president, Big Doc Emerson was the big dean and a rather outstanding person in every respect. I will never forget him telling two or three bad boys who had had a run-in with the law that "a young man can still drink and be a gentleman." A lecture from him really took hold, I can assure you.

After entering the freshman class the grades of this scholar began to go downhill. I became more enamored of football and track than with study, and after World War I started, I was glad to get out of BoCat's calculus and enter the Navy. I enlisted in February, 1918, and was called up the following month.

No matter where you go your sins will find you out. The first fellow I ran into when I entered the Officers School in Charleston was none other than the old sub, Morgan McNeel, of Marietta.

My first experience with Ensign McNeel was when he was commissioned. He couldn't wait to put that ensign's uniform on. Just as soon as he was sworn in, he rushed down to his room, put on his uniform and came into our class. He thought that some one would call attention, but instead a big boo went up. McNeel, in his hurry to give us a run around, had put his shoulder boards on backwards. Then another time, I was tussling with McNeel and somehow or another managed to throw him, I was really giving him a licking when he said "Griffin, you better get up from here or I'll put my coat on and call you to attention."

Talking about McNeel reminds me—he went out for baseball. He was a pretty good ball player and made the first squad. You know how Old Man Heisman was. The minute you did something wrong, he would take you off the Varsity Squad and send you back to the Scrubs. Well, in a practice game McNeel was picked off second and right away he was back on the Scrubs, and when the team left on the weekend to play Sewanee McNeel was left behind. McNeel had attended Sewanee Military Academy and knew all about the dances at the University, which were real ones, so he packed his bag, took his dinner coat and left for the dances. He was set for a big time. When the team arrived Burghard, the center fielder, was taken ill. Old Man Heisman was up against it, so he was casting around trying to solve this problem when one of the fellows said "Coach, McNeel is up here to attend the dances." Well, that was enough; Coach ran McNeel down, gave him Burghard's uniform, and McNeel had to play every game and didn't make a single dance. That was too much for that Tea Hound.

After World War I many of the fellows returned to college and tried to take up where they left off. Old Griffin gave it a try, and before he knew it he was out of school. He thought he was a hot-shot sprinter and that he could make the Olympic Team in 1920. The result was that he didn't even get to try, but he did bust out of college. Well, things looked bad but he was lucky. It looked like we would be short on halfbacks in 1920 so I entered summer school and finally made it back. I knew I had the Varsity made, but lo and behold really never made the squad. I was called in by Coach Heisman and asked would I help coach. That was my downfall.

Again, though, hard luck overtook me. My Dad had a serious setback in business, and I had to drop out and go to work. Suddenly during that summer Alex was made head coach when Heisman resigned to go to Penn as head coach. Alex was without a staff, so he wired me and asked would I come back and coach the freshman team that fall. I talked it over with my boss and he said, yes, that would be fine. He told me it would be a great experience and to report back for work on the second of January, 1921. Well, Mr. Bird has had a long wait. I re-entered school and have been around here more or less since.

I would like to say one thing and that is this: The Georgia Tech alumni have been good to me over the years and I will never be able to repay them, but I will never forget.

The First Georgia Game

This game, famous in song and story, always bears repeating, so to start our little book off I am taking the liberty of giving you my version.

The first football team at Tech was an informal one in 1892; I know only two or three of these men, namely Mr. Merry, founder of the Merry Brick Company, and Mr. Ed Werner of Atlanta. Mr. Merry was from Augusta. The coach was Professor Frank Spain of the Math Department, who also played fullback. No rules in those days. I also had the good fortune of knowing Professor Spain, who came by to see me about 20 years ago.

As the story goes, the Tech team was practicing one afternoon (there was no Grant Field at that time, not even the old field known as Tech Flats which occupied the site of Grant Field and which was partly built by the students). There was a creek running through that property; in fact it is still there, known as Tanyard Creek, but it now runs under Grant Field.

Such being the case the only level place around was the property next to the YMCA that is now owned by the government as a part of the Techwood Housing Project. This property was surrounded by a real ghetto. By the way, Techwood was the first government project in America, and was built by Raymond Jones, Class of 1916.

Going back to practice, the boys were struggling along, when up rode a young man on horseback. In 1893, with only a few cars in Atlanta, everyone rode in buggies, carriages, or on horseback. The young man sat on his horse for a while, then he dismounted. The Tech boys struck up a conversation with him and found that he had played football four years while in college, I believe at Harvard, and they also found out that he was a second lieutenant in the Army stationed at Fort McPherson.

Well, one thing led to another. Not having much to do, since the country was undergoing one of its peaceful periods, the young lieutenant came out the next morning and enrolled at Tech. The lieutenant's biographer says that he signed up for one course—woodshop—and that he was a much better football player than he was a cabinet maker.

Well, the season rolled along and Tech had lost one of the three games played that year to a little school called St. Albans of Washington, D.C. They had tied Auburn 0 to 0 and the season seemed to be at an end when all of a sudden they received a challenge from the Bulldogs for a game to be played at Athens.

Georgia was undefeated at the time, and had an open game and wanted to use the Techs as a doormat and a good workout before they met Vanderbilt, the other undefeated team in the South at that time.

The day of the trip to Athens rolled around. The Tech team boarded the train for the classic city for their drubbing. But somehow or another things went wrong and it was a preview of 1927, when the Techs defeated the great Georgia Dream and Wonder Team. The young lieutenant who was playing guard ran wild. They were playing the T formation. The quarterback would take the snap, spin around, and the right guard would pull out of the line and dash around left end or left tackle. When the dust subsided, Tech had scored 28 points and the Bulldogs 6. What a great victory.

The whistle blew and then the fun started. Rocks began to fly and the Techs lit out in a dead run for the railroad station, the lieutenant in the lead. The race kept on, and many of the Techs were passed by the crowd, who were after that hated lieutenant, that ringer, but he sped on, leaving his pursuers behind. Finally he made the train and safety, the others straggled in, and the train got underway for home and mother, but bad luck was still following. The train broke down about halfway between Athens and Atlanta, so the team landed in Gate City on a freight. They finally made it back to the campus with a great victory, and with a new cry: "To Hell with Georgia."

Ferd Kaufman, who was a substitute on the 1893 team, said

while he was in Washington on business he decided to go by and call on the young lieutenant, then Major General Leonard Wood, Chief of Staff of the United States Army.

Ferd said the first thing the general did after greeting him was to reach in the bottom right hand drawer of his desk, bring out a picture of the 1893 team and ask about each man on the squad, remembering each by name. Ferd left after a most enjoyable visit.

General Wood later became Governor General of Cuba, and later Governor General of the Philippines, and was joobed out of the nomination for the Presidency of the United States by the Republican Party at that time.

The 1892 team was really a bear for punishment, losing to Mercer 12 to 0, Vanderbilt 20 to 10, and to Auburn 26 to 0, but they started the game at Tech which has meant so much to all of us.

Rambling Wreck

There have been many stories about the birth of the great Georgia Tech battle song, our beloved *Rambling Wreck*. Here is one version that might be of interest. This story was also told by Ferd Kaufman.

We all know that Tech played Auburn at Auburn in 1970 and, as the newspapers say, for the first time in a long time, but back in 1892 or 1893 one of these two games was played at Auburn. As Mr. Kaufman told the tale, the team was riding down to Auburn on the train with very little to do and as young collegians are and always have been rather inventive, the subject came up as to a school song. Someone thought about the tune—it was an old English drinking song—and the Techs sat around and made up the words to *Rambling Wreck*. I am sorry to say there are many more verses, not fit for publication in a family journal, but the old song has been with us nigh a hundred years. It is probably the most famous college song in the world. Now I don't know how true this story is, but I'm sure Mr. Kaufman knew what he was talking about. There are several other versions that no one can prove, so the writer carries on with this. The song was first orchestrated by Mike Greenblatt, our first band leader, who later became a prominent Atlanta businessman. The present orchestration was brought out by Frank Roman, who succeeded Mike and made a few changes that he felt helped the song. Mike was here with us for many years and his famous statement, "believe me kiddo," was popular around Tech.

Tech's Greatest Student

There is one man who has been a student at Tech for many years whose record as a student has never been approached. And no one ever will approach his record, because according to the last information from the Registrar's office he still has 3,000 hours to complete before graduation. This wonderful lad is none other than one George P. Burdell, whose name has become a tradition at Tech. My first encounter with this gentleman occurred several years ago when I began to receive thanks from various friends for the subscription to *Fortune* with which I had presented them one Christmas. I fell in a faint and couldn't get a letter off to Time, Inc. fast enough. Since then he has kept various people on the campus and off quite busy over the years trying to keep up with his many activities, particularly the society editors who have hoped that old Griffin would wake up to the fact that the only way to keep up with this lad is to have two or three agents working undercover at all times.

Even our former Governor has had his experiences with George. One night while speaking to the Tech Alumni of Atlanta, Governor Maddox said that while running the Pickrick Restaurant he was quite impressed with the Tech students who patronized his restaurant. Their honesty, patience and manners made a deep impression on him and when he found it necessary to help out a lad in distress, he never failed to repay him. But he went on to say that in every barrel of apples there was always a rotten one, and he wanted the Tech Alumni to help him run down one George P. Burdell who still owed him $9.90.

George knew everyone it seems. His first victims were the society editors of our Atlanta papers. Each year for several years a big write-up appeared on the society pages of our local papers about the big ball he was giving for the Debs of Atlanta plus their escorts and friends. Now you had better not mention George P. Burdell to them.

The insurance people at times have become quite confused over Mr. Burdell and even recently he just about ran a new insurance man crazy trying to locate him and sell him a policy before he graduated. When I was Dean of Students, many times it was necessary to write book companies, etc. about our friend. He never rested.

Finally it looked as if he was about to leave school because the computer people had moved into the registration picture here at Tech and it seemed impossible for him to beat the machine and register for class. The faculty heaved a sigh of relief, especially the new men on the staff. Every once in awhile he would receive a passing grade in a course, which always proved embarrassing to the guilty instructor because his older pals wouldn't let him forget it. Of course George also had his record of failures, which were almost as bad.

A notice appeared in a column in *The Atlanta Journal* about George's idea of dropping out because Tech would not allow him to register. This really brought about a commotion on campus. How the students did it no one knows but a few days after registration Mr. Burdell had registered for 3,000 hours, which assured his attendance at Tech for many more years. Never challenge the Tech boys.

D. M. and Alex

If there was ever a pair of characters on this campus, D. M. Smith and W. A. Alexander certainly filled the bill. At one time they lived together in Knowles in the only room in the building with a bath. At least they didn't have to go outside to take a shower. One day I saw Doc Smith on the campus and asked how he and his roommate were getting along. He took the bait and said he would like to get rid of him, and when I asked why, he said "he only owns one pair of sheets and one pair of pajamas. When the sheets are in the laundry he uses his pajamas, and when his pajamas are in the laundry he sleeps between the sheets. I would like to have a fellow that at least had one more pair of sheets and one more pair of pajamas."

At that time the rooms were lighted by oil lamps and every lad was required to have an oil can. Well this was not too bad, but as luck would have it there was a saloon at the corner of North Avenue and Marietta, "The First and Last Chance" The first saloon coming into Atlanta from the north and the last leaving Atlanta for the Smith and Wesson Line. As a result, many of the students had two oil cans—one for the beer and the other for the kerosene. Alex said, every once in a while someone would get the cans mixed up and have kerosene in his beer can. But they drank it anyhow because money in those days was hard to come by.

D.M. was a great one. Here is the masterpiece Doc wrote to thank Roddy Garrison for a valuable Christmas gift.

Dear Roddy:
    Without lowering the standards of Georgia Tech, I hereby assign you two grades of "A"; one is for your excellent portrayal of Santa Claus. The other is for the rare and expert choice of the brand— Old # 7! This was the favorite of my grandfather and of my father. It has been my choice since infancy! It was also dear to the heart of Coach Alex, who said # 7 made a coach "Generous in victory and magnificent in defeat!"
    And, finally, (let us approach this case reverently) Old # 7 was the life-long choice of Dr. Coon! It was a bottle of this outstanding brand that, in the early days of prohibition, was discovered in Dr. Coon's room and caused him to be hauled into court!* It was at the "trial" for illegal possession that the prosecutor, irritated by Dr. Coon's sarcasm, roared out "do you know who I am?" and received the immortal reply, "no, but I know *what* you are!" As you may recall, the judge apologized to Dr. Coon and ordered his quart of # 7 (*quart* mind you, not a fifth) restored to him! The whole affair, in my book, was priceless.
    Just one sad note—I missed seeing you when you made delivery.

But my loss was Mrs. Bancock's gain, for she enjoyed talking to you very much.

With thanks for your gracious Christmas remembrance, and hoping to see you soon, I am

Sincerely,
"D.M."

P.S. The mercury is falling! A mark of 10 is predicted! I shall make me a "Tom & Jerry" with # 7!

Editorial note: See pp. 112 for a full account of this incident.

Poor Old Burdell

One year Alex conceived the idea that he would make me the trainer of the football team. I was track coach at the time and it seems that this job usually went along with his work, although it might be the fact (most likely) they were trying to save a little money. Anyhow, neither Alex nor the writer knew too much about the job and at times we didn't think that we would be able to make it on Saturday.

I remember our treatment for charley horses (the very thing you shouldn't do) was to have Bill Fincher, who was tackle on the team at the time, take his strong fingers and rub it out. We would get the lad back after two or three weeks.

Well, anyhow, Burdell, one of the few Latin boys to make the Tech Varsity football squad, came to me with a bad back. I called Alex and asked him what I should do for Burdell's back. He said put a piece of Cathardie's plaster on it and tell him to see you tomorrow. Well, Burdell came up to the little place we had just above the dressing room under the old West Stand, ready to be treated. I took a roll of the plaster and cut a piece twelve inches square, taped it down tight, told Burdell to check with me the next day, and went merrily off to have a date that evening.

Old Dr. Cox and Fuzzy White were running the old drug store at North Avenue and Luckie at the time and they stayed open 'til eleven each night to catch that stray nickel, sitting around two thirds of the time doing nothing other than shooting the breeze with Alex and some of the boys.

Finally, Dr. Cox closed up and started home. After awhile he

(Continued on page 25)

The 1916-17 version of the I-formation at Tech. Right to left: Judy Harlan, Strup Strupper, and Albert Hill lead the way for Joe Guyon.

The famous A. R. (Buck) Flowers, captain of Tech's 1920 National Championship team—said by many to be Tech's greatest halfback.

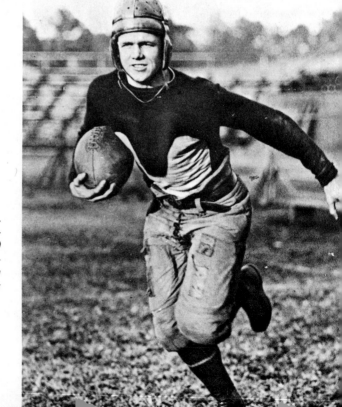

The 1920 team running onto Grant Field before the famous Tech-Centre game, which Tech won 24-0.

C. D. (Dummy) LeBey, Griffin's roommate, who was named All-Southern in 1920.

Two-time All-American tackle and end Bill Fincher, one of the many stars of Tech's 1920 "Golden Tornado" team.

Ed Hamm (left), former holder of the world record, the Olympic record, and winner in the Southern Conference for three straight years in the 100 and 220 yard runs. Captain Welchel (right), another Olympic runner from Tech.

"Father" Lumpkin

"Stumpy" Thomason, owner of the famous bear.

Peter Pund, Captain of the famous Rose Bowl Football Team.

The real "World's greatest Golfer" —Robert T. (Bob) Jones, Georgia Tech B.S.M.E. 1922.

passed a lad all bent over, holding the back of his trousers away
from his back, stumbling along trying to make his way to the
drug store. Doc asked him what was the matter with him. Burdell
said he was dying. Doc said come down to the store and we will
see just what is wrong. He laid Burdell on a table, took the tape
off, and there he was with a blister on his back twelve inches
square and about one-half inch high. Doc finally got him to his
room and called Alex the next morning. Alex took him to the
dressing room, stripped Burdell, and laid him on a bench. He got
a bucket of hot water, poured some baking soda in and stirred
it up. He took a pair of scissors, punctured the blister, took a
sponge that had been in the hot soda water, and put it on the
wound. Well, after a three-week stay in the infirmary Burdell
came back.

A little later Burdell was hurt again, and I told him to come
on up and I would take care of him. He said, wagging his finger
as the Latin boys do, No. No. No. He had had enough of Doctor
Griffin.

A Saying of Father Lumpkin

All of us remember old Father Lumpkin, the great fullback of
the 1928 National Championship team. It is too bad Father did
not play his last two years at Tech. There is no question that he
would have made All-American and probably would have become
the greatest fullback the South had ever seen. Father had one saying that he used many times. When the going got tough and Tech
was stymied, Father would take time out and say "give me the
ball, I'll fire both barrels at them." And he would.

All of us know the story about Father and the freshman coach
at that time. In an interview with the coach he was asked what
position he played. Father said fullback, and the coach said "I
have a fullback." Father said "I know you have; here he is right
here." A little later the coach went to Alex and said he was having trouble with Lumpkin, that he kept on insisting that he was
a fullback. The coach wanted to play him at tackle. Alex said

"well, we are going to scrimmage the freshmen for the first time today and after the scrimmage I will talk to you."

The scrimmage took place and Father just about laid the varsity out for the season. After it was all over Alex said "Coach, I believe Father has more sense than you do."

A Visit to the Steel Mill

One day during the summer Alex was sitting in his office scribbling away when in walked Frank Thomas, the famous Alabama coach. After their greetings and shooting of the breeze, Frank asked Alex if he had a boy working out at the Atlantic Steel Company and if so he would like permission to talk to him. Alex said that it would be perfectly all right to go right out to the main office, and they would arrange a meeting.

Frank was dressed in a beautiful white suit, white shoes, etc., just as if he had come from a band box. Mr. Nat Harrison, whose sons were managers of the football team, was vice-president of the Atlantic Steel Company, so each year we would go out and get him to give some of the lads a summer job, especially some boy we didn't want anyone to bother.

Anyhow, Frank went out to the mill. Everyone was as nice as they could be to the famous coach. Finally a messenger came in and told Frank that the lad was working for Mr. Russell Bobbitt, superintendent of the open hearth. They found Mr. Bobbitt and gave him the message about talking to the lad.

Mr. Bobbitt went looking for the lad and left Frank standing there in front of the hot furnaces. After about twenty minutes he came back and said he was sorry but the young man had been transferred to the converters.

The messenger offered to take the coach over to Mr. Lang, the superintendent. Bob had been an All-American Guard on two of the great Tech teams and had played in the Tech band, so Frank was really getting the VIP treatment.

They found Mr. Lang, and while he went looking for the lad Frank was left standing in front of the converters. Bob was gone about fifteen minutes. By that time Frank's collar had wilted, the beautiful white suit was covered with cinders and finally, in disgust, he left. He came back to Alex's office looking like something the cat had dragged in and said "Alex, I was just a damn fool. I knew you were not going to let me see that boy."

The Longest Punt in History

One day back in the early twenties Tech was playing Oglethorpe at Grant Field. Tech was ahead by about twenty points when Alex sent word in to punt the ball. The ball was then resting on about the Tech 15-yard line. This didn't sit too well with the team members, so after a timeout they decided to run the ball. The play was called and Tech gained about 15 yards.

Alex was rather upset, took the quarterback out and sent in another man to punt. The same thing happened; the boys ran the ball, this time up to about the fifty.

Well, about this time Alex was fuming, so he took this quarterback out and sent in the third man to punt. This was a little too much; the team ran the ball again, this time down to the Oglethorpe eight-yard line.

Alex was then about ready to explode. He finally called Don Hartford, the lowliest of the scrubs whom he allowed to dress and sit on the bench each Saturday as more or less a reward for his faithful services. He said "Hartford, if you ever want to play football at Tech you go in there and punt that ball—I don't care where it is." Don went in, called for a punt, and then a riot took place.

Don finally called the team together (he later became one of the top officials of the DuPont Co.) and told them he was going to punt no matter what they had to say. He repeated what Coach Alex had said so, with much grumbling, the team lined up for the punt.

Pratt Rather, who was a fine punter, got into position (Pratt later became president and chairman of the board of the Southeastern Gas Corporation). The ball was snapped and away went the punt. This was the days before the concrete stands at Grant Field and Tech had a wooden stadium seating about 27,000 people, which was naturally much lower than it is now. It was a beautiful punt, for about 50 yards, high enough that the ends could well cover the ball, but as luck would have it the ball landed on North Avenue. Pratt had kicked clean out of the field.

Things like this, though, never work out as planned. Alex felt the team needed work on defense, but circumstances didn't permit. After the tremendous punt, Oglethorpe was given the ball as a touchback.

They lined up for the usual four plays and didn't make the first down, so Oglethorpe lined up to punt. The ball was snapped and the punt was blocked. Jess Cauldwell fell on it for a touchdown, which ended all of Alex's plan.

Another funny thing happened about this punt. Many years later Howard Ector, who was acting as Alumni Secretary, was speaking at an Alumni meeting in Virginia. He told this story, describing the dirty little scrub who went into the game to obey orders. As he went on, everyone started laughing. The laughter kept increasing, which really confused the speaker, and finally after tremendous applause he sat down. They then told him Mr. Hartford, who was the honored guest, was the dirty little quarterback he was talking about.

Bob Randolph's Tooth

One cold, dreary day, Tech was playing Notre Dame at Grant Field. The wind was blowing, the temperature was below thirty, everyone including the players was uncomfortable and, all in all, it was a most unsatisfactory day.

Coach Alexander looked up all of a sudden. There was a lull in the proceedings and there was Bob Randolph running around on all fours sniffing the ground like a dog. This went on for a minute or two with everyone standing around on the field.

Finally Alex received permission to go out on the field. He walked up to Randolph and asked what in the world was the matter. Bob looked up, pointed to the inside of his mouth and said "ahhhhhhh." Alex again asked him what was the matter. Bob pointed again and said "AHHHHHHH."

Once more this happened, then Alex finally noticed that Bob's front tooth was gone and the nerve was hanging out. Every time the cold air hit it, it about knocked Randolph out.

Alex was chewing gum. He reached in his mouth, took it out, wadded it up, stuck it on Bob's nerve, and told him to go ahead and start playing again. Bob told the coach that he just couldn't play a whole game against Notre Dame on one stick of gum, so Alex came back to the bench, gave all hands a stick of gum, and told them to chew away. Then about every five minutes a freshman manager would rush out on the field and stick another piece of gum on Randolph's nerve.

The Giant with the Voice
of a Little Girl

One day back in the twenties one of Tech's great championship teams was playing Davidson College. Davidson was not in Tech's class, but had one of the hardest fighting teams that ever played on Grant Field. In fact that is where Buck Flowers was in college before he transferred to Tech. Well, two funny things happened in that game, the first being the outstanding play of a lad by the name of Siad from Assyria who was playing guard for Davidson. In fact, we used to kid Bill Fincher about Siad having taught him how to play the game. Siad is now a prominent doctor in Palm Beach, Florida. Anyhow, there was another guard on the Davidson team, a little lad giving all he had at all times. He was across from Bill Fincher. Bill, as you know, had the misfortune to lose one of his eyes as a youth, which did not keep him from making All-American.

As the game progressed (Bill had forgotten to take his artificial eye out before the game) the young guard for Davidson was relieved and he came out of the game. Bob Fetzer, the Davidson coach, said "well, Tom, you were not doing too well out there." Tom said "Coach, I knocked the guy's eye out, what more can you expect me to do."

The game moved along; Tech was supposed to win by at least 28 points. The game started and the first quarter ended 0 to 0. The second quarter ended still 0 to 0. The third quarter ended with the same score. By that time the coaches, the players, the stands and the boys on the bench really became excited. It looked as if the great Tech team was about to mar a great season by tying little Davidson.

Finally Dummy LeBey, who was acting captain, took time out to talk to the team and try to build up a little pep and enthusiasm. The fellows began to talk it up in an attempt to throw off the lazy spirit that had somehow developed during the game. Everyone had his say except Homer Whelchel, who was playing fullback that day because Judy Harlan, who was All-Southern at the time, was injured. Homer was about the quietest fellow who ever attended Tech. He hardly ever spoke, and when he did he talked exactly like a girl. This is how he got his nickname, Calliope.

Everyone else was talking and jabbering, trying his best to stir up the right spirit, except Whelchel. He stood there listening but saying nothing. Finally Dummy spoke up and told Homer to say something. Homer then threw his head back, stood erect, and in his little girlish voice said "let's go, boys."

It's hard to describe in words just how it sounded, but all of a sudden the whole team was hollering and laughing and some were rolling on the ground. Finally the time was up and they went back at it. This speech of Homer's did the work, because the team got together and soon had nine points and saved a fine record for the old school.

Where Do You Put That Two?

Back in the old days, a lad was found in the mountains of Tennessee who passed all the requirements of an All-Southern fullback. We had to have him here at Tech, but as it turned out and as it has turned out here with us for many years, he did not have the credits.

The authorities were finally prevailed upon and a ruling was handed down that if he passed the four required entrance examinations he would be allowed to enter.

Tutors were employed and they went to work with a must-do schedule. Things rocked along fairly well until the exam in algebra came around. Alex, who was teaching math at the time, decided that he had better get his fine Italian hand into the situation, so the night before the exam he went by Burdell's room in Knowles and sat down with him for three or four hours. He told Burdell that they had gone over everything that they might ask so was there anything now that was not understood. Burdell said no, that he was ready. Alex told him good night, got up to leave, and just as he was about to close the door, Burdell spoke up and asked him to wait just a minute that there was one thing he wanted to know.

Alex came back and sat down while Burdell picked up a sheet of paper and a pencil and drew an X on the paper, in fact two X's. He placed a 2 in front of one X, and a small 2 over the top of the right hand corner of the other X. He then said "Coach, you know that X, don't you?" Alex of course said yes, that he knew the X. Burdell then said "why is it they sometimes put the two in front of the X and sometimes on top of the X? Why don't they settle on a regular place? If they would I know I would pass."

Well, today he's still following that mule over the hills of Tennessee.

Stone Mountain Ain't Nothing But a Foul Ball

When Tech was invited to the Rose Bowl game in 1929, the newspapers in Atlanta held a popularity contest. After much excitement and thousands of votes, our old friend Tubby Walton won out.

Tubby was a great favorite of the Tech boys. He would come out to their pep meetings and speak to them before a big game. Tubby really lived up to his name in those days; I can see him now sitting on the stage at the YMCA, on two chairs, waiting to speak.

All kinds of stories are told about Tubby's trip. As all of us know he ran a restaurant here in Atlanta for years. I am afraid Tubby made very little in his venture, because during the depresion of the thirties he fed thousands of fellows which, I am sure, kept him broke all the time. Anyhow, as the story goes, Tubby was afraid that they would not feed him well on the train so he carried along two suitcases full of fried chicken to see him through the three or four day trip. He made it all right.

After this famous victory, Alex took the boys into Mexico for a day or so and then on the way back stayed two days at the Grand Canyon. The first afternoon there Tubby wandered off by himself at about sunset. He stood there on the rim of the canyon, enthralled by the beautiful scene. About that time Alex walked up tapped him on the back and said "Tubby, what do you think of that?" Without a moment's hesitation, Tubby turned around and said "Coach, Stone Mountain ain't nothing but a foul ball."

Babes in the Woods

When the eligibility of Buck Flowers and Griffin ran out Coach Alex offered me the job as freshman coach and Buck the job as assistant backfield coach at the wonderful salary of $75 a month. Don't laugh, because this was back in 1920-21 when money was real money and $75 was not to be sneered at.

Anyhow, that $75 looked like a million to us, so nothing would do except to run down to George Muse's store, still about the leading men's store in Atlanta, and buy about $150 worth of clothes. We were really going to knock the gal's eyes out.

Little did we realize that a day of reckoning would soon come. The first of the month rolled around, the bills arrived, and our hearts sank. We went to Alex's office on the second floor of the YMCA to talk the matter over. While we waited on him to return to his office nothing occurred to us that would solve the situation, so we sat there holding our heads and wondering what would happen next. Finally the door opened and Alex walked in. He greeted us, then we just lapsed into a period of silence. Alex asked what was the matter with us, and at first we said nothing. He then said he knew darn well something was wrong and that we might just as well get it off our chest.

What a welcome sound. We gave him the full load. After listening to our story he said he was going down tomorrow and pay the bills, and that we were not going to get any more money the rest of the year. If we needed money we had to go and see him. This was terrible, but to get out from under we agreed.

It was a tough life. I can see old Flowers now, walking in and asking the coach if he could have a dollar to have a date. Alex would say "I'll give you fifty cents" and Buck would tell him he couldn't have a date on fifty cents. Alex would say "yes you can. Street car fare is 5 cents; that's 10 cents to get you to town. The movies are 10 cents; that's 20 cents to see the show. Street car fare back is 10 cents more for the both of you, and that leaves you a dime to buy your girl a Coca-Cola." Buck would take the fifty cents, and with his head hanging would go out and do the best he could.

One day I found the old book where Alex kept our accounts, and I turned it over to the library. Under Flowers you would find "Date—50 cents" plus a few other items. Under Griffin—I didn't waste my money on the gals—you would see, "Pajamas—$1.00," "Shirts—$1.50," etc. At the end though we were rich.

The World's Greatest Score

It seems that stories about Tech's famous victory in 1916 will never fail to be of interest. As we all know Tech won the game 222-0. (O. K. Armstrong wrote it up for the *Reader's Digest* with the title "The Funniest Football Game Ever Played.") The game really only lasted about 40 minutes since the last quarter was cut to seven minutes, plus the fact that the first three quarters were only twelve minutes long.

Cumberland, reviewing the history a little, was Southern Champion in 1903, 1904, 1905, and if I am not mistaken, again in 1908, but I can't be sure of this. Anyhow, Cumberland had had her day. She was scheduled by Coach Heisman, and offered a guarantee, I believe, of $500. Since there was a written contract covering the game Cumberland authorities, after deciding to give up football, felt that they had better go ahead and play it.

Several of the Cumberland fellows managed to get together a group, among them a gentleman by the name of Dugat, who was one of the ringleaders. Dugat had played two games of football in his life, so you can see that he was a real experienced hand at the game.

Anyhow, 19 men were brought together and several practices were held. The day of the game was soon upon them, so they started to Atlanta to collect money. On the way they stopped in Nashville and tried to recruit two or three men from the Vanderbilt squad, but with a night game coming up the Vandy boys had to decline. Well, our friends arrived in Atlanta ready for the fray. There were several things of interest that happened. For one there is only one picture of the game as far as anyone can remember. Second, there were not over five or six thousand people in the stands—the students plus maybe 3,500 others. The game started and Tech was off to the races. The score began to mount. Under the old rules a man, after entering the game and returning to the bench, could not return until the start of the next quarter. Since Cumberland only had about sixteen men, Tech waived the substitution rule and put in what is now known as the "platoon system."

A right funny thing happened about this. Late in the game one of the Cumberland lads came over and took a seat on the Tech bench. Coach Heisman finally noticed him and told him he was on the wrong bench. The lad said no, he was on the right bench. Coach Heisman walked away and came by later and again told him he was on the wrong bench. The lad again said he was on the right bench. Finally Coach Heisman came back and said *"son, you are on the wrong bench!"* The lad said "no, Coach, I'm on the right bench. If I go back over there they'll put me in again. I've been in five times already and that's enough." So there he sat.

Another story made famous by George Allen is the one about a player fumbling the ball and hollering "fall on it!" One of his pals yelled back "you fall on it, you fumbled it!"

One rather interesting thing was the fact that Jim Preas, one of the Tech guards, kicked 18 consecutive goals after touchdown in the first half. Bill Fincher came in and kicked the rest without missing. I asked Bill the other day how many he kicked, and he said he didn't know but Jim kicked 18 in the first half. Not being very good in math, he said, he was never able to figure the number he kicked.

One of the most amusing things was Canty Alexander's touchdown. The preceding Saturday Tech had played Mercer and won by a big score. Canty had played on the team four years and never made a touchdown. He was crying in his beer over that fact, and said he wanted to make one since it was his last year. This deal was framed up before the game.

When Tech was well ahead at the end of the game, Strupper was to take the ball and, just before scoring, was to put the ball on the one-yard line even though he could have run over the goal easily.

Well, Strupper did this. He ran 30 or 40 yards with the ball, stopped, placed the ball on the one-yard line, and things were ready. Canty came into the backfield. The ball was snapped, and the Mercer boys came through like Assyrians and just about killed Canty. The Tech linemen just moved out of the way and let them through. This they did for four downs; by that time Canty was back about the five-yard line and all Tech had was a terribly disgruntled Canty Alexander, who was really upset with his pals.

Well, before the Cumberland game came around it was decided to do the same thing again. So Strupper, after a long run, placed the ball on the one-yard line. Canty was brought back and he tried again. The same thing took place, but lo and behold Canty fumbled the ball, picked it up, and ran across for his score. You could run with fumbles in those days. The chagrined people were the linemen, because Canty had stolen a march on them.

As Bill Fincher said, the Cumberland boys had a lot of guts. Many had never played in a game before, but they stuck it out, swallowed their pride, and finished the job.

In 1956 Furman Bisher, now Sports Editor of *The Atlanta Journal,* suggested that we get the Cumberland and Tech boys who had played in the famous game together for a reunion. The game had become famous, and along with Dugat from Cumberland and one or two of us here at Tech, the reunion was held. It was a grand and glorious party. Practically all of the Tech team returned, and six of the Cumberland group came along with the president.

Cumberland won this battle. All of the Cumberland men were asked to say a few words; all were solicitors general, lawyers, preachers, etc., and they laid the audience in the aisles with their wonderful oratory. The Tech men were called on to say a few words. Every speech was about as follows "gee this is wonderful; lets do it again five years from now." So I guess you can call the game a standoff.

The Ghost of Peters Park

Stumpy's bear, as you know, had a home under the East Stand when he was not operating with the boys, and in the evenings he was chained up to keep him from wandering around the neighborhood. On occasion he was not chained properly or managed to break his chain, and when he did, particularly in the evenings, he liked to wander down through Peters Park which at that time was quite a nice residential section.

One night one of the ladies heard a noise on her back porch, and she got up and went back to the kitchen to investigate. She looked out the back door, which was half glass, and saw this terrible monster trying to get into her refrigerator. She let out a terrible scream and fainted dead away. Her old man was reading the sports page and, being deeply engrossed, didn't make a move. The daughter, realizing that something had happened to her mother, rushed to the kitchen, saw this terrible apparition, and keeled over with a scream.

By this time the father realized something out of the ordinary had happened. He walked back to the kitchen and saw his wife and daughter on the floor. He glanced out the kitchen door and there was Mr. Bear. He rushed to the telephone, called the police department, and told the lieutenant that there was a bear on his back porch. The lieutenant scoffed at him and said "sir, you have been drinking; go back and take another look." The gentleman meekly returned to the kitchen, came back, and said "he's still there and big as a house." By that time the lieutenant realized what was going on, because old brother bear was always giving them a little excitement. He called the patrol car and told them Stumpy's bear was loose again down in Peters Park, to go down and pick him up, which was not hard to do. Mr. Bear was returned home.

A Couple of Shorties

When Sam Murray was playing fullback on the team back in 1925 and 1926 he was rooming with Karl Nixon and Shorty McLellelan. Shorty was later manager of the football team. Sam and Karl were always playing tricks on Shorty, and one day they nailed the door up on him in Knowles. It was night and Shorty couldn't get in. Finally he decided he would get even with those two devils, so he got a bucket, filled it with water, borrowed a chair, and dumped the bucket of water through the transom. He did this about a dozen times, and finally Karl and Sam opened the door to let him in. Much to Shorty's dismay he saw his trunk, a big, old-fashioned one, full of water. His Sunday best was floating around.

That was too much. He knew of a room that had an empty

bed down the hall, so he immediately moved out. Well, he was
gone about a week and while Sam and Karl were out one day
he moved back in. The guy he roomed with at the time had not
had a bath in over a month, one of the first hippies, and he
couldn't stand it any longer. But we are happy to say that after
that Sam and Karl let things alone. After graduating from Tech
Sam attended medical school. Many years later, when Shorty
needed a serious operation, Sam was his first thought; Sam went
down and pulled him through.

A Case of Mistaken Identity

Tech and Georgia were playing the annual Thanksgiving game.
It was a cold muddy day, just a quagmire since this was before
Grant Field was properly drained and Tech didn't have a cover.
The game rocked along. Lefty Eubanks, later varsity captain,
was playing tackle for Tech and his old high school pal, Allen
Shi, was playing tackle opposite him. One had gone to Tech, the
other to Georgia. You couldn't tell one player from another, and
all of a sudden I saw Shi haul off and cool one of his Georgia
teammates. I thought this was rather peculiar, so the next day
when Shi and Lefty came by the office to see me I asked Allen
"what in the world did you want to knock that Georgia player
out for?" He looked at me with a sheepish grin and said "Mr.
Griffin, I thought it was Lefty."

Bunch's Creek

When the writer returned to Tech to help Alex with his re-
cruiting problems back in the early thirties (1930-31), Alex had
decided to make a radical change in the scholarship setup here
at Tech. He called me in and told me that he was going to try
a plan for five years that in the long run might cost both of
us our jobs. The plan was a loan setup taken up with the parents
of the young men in whom the Athletic Association was inter-

ested. This meant that after getting the prospect somewhat interested you then went to the parent and talked to him about the advantages of such a plan. This left the young man in question in such a position that he would not consider himself a hired hand, but in the long run would pay for his education.

First we had to select certain schools from which we would try to draw prospects. We had to have young men who could pass the work here at Tech, and since there were so many three-year high schools at that time our field was rather limited. Second, it took some mighty high-powered selling to get a lad to come to Tech. I know I used to take Dr. George Sparks with me on many of the trips. Dr. Sparks would talk to the parent and I would give the lad the benefit of my great knowledge. If you remember, Dr. Sparks was head of the Industrial Management School for many years, and was later President of Georgia State College where he made a name that will live in the annals of education in our state.

There was a great football player at McCallie School, Decatur Jackson Phillips of Waynesville, N.C., who later came to Tech and became captain and All-Southern fullback. Things had boiled down to Duke and Georgia Tech. We knew the time had come, so we gave him a call.

We jumped in our car and made our way to Waynesville to Jack's home along with Roy Mundorff.

Jack was not there, but he had left word with his Dad to have Roy and myself come to the top of Black Mountain, I believe was the name, and he would meet us there. A small gasoline car would be making its way to the top of the mountain that afternoon, and if we would be there around 3:00 p.m. it would take us up.

Well, Mundorff and I made our way to the foot of the mountain and the car was there with a lady and a man who turned out to be the crew. Mundorff and I boarded the little flat-bottom car and away we went. We passed an old mountaineer carrying a long rifle on his shoulder, who said he was going to the top of the mountain to find some of his cattle that had broken loose.

After about a mile the belt on the little gasoline engine began to slip, and we finally came to a full stop. Well, a few minor repairs were made and Roy and I jumped on, but instead of the young lady getting aboard she began to push us. After a while the engine caught up and away we went. The higher we went the more the belt began to slip again. The girl and the man jumped off and made the repairs, and the girl pushed again. When this happened the third time, I told Roy I just couldn't stand having the girl push us off. So we both jumped off and started pushing. I will never forget what she said "you city boys get back on there—you'll get hurt." What about that!

We finally made it to the top, and Jack and one of his friends were there to greet us. They had made arrangements to take us on a fishing trip the next morning in Bunch's Creek, and they put us up in an old shack that had been used by the woodsmen several years before. We were tired, so decided to go to bed about dusk. Well, we were soon awake again. We made a light and looked down at ourselves and the old bedding, and if there was one flea on us there were a million. For years the sheep had been sleeping under the bedroom, and the fleas had taken over. We hurriedly left the building and went outside to make a pallet under the trees.

At the crack of day we got up, fixed our fishing gear, and went 4,000 feet down the mountain to Bunch's Creek. We began to fish in the pools we passed as we made our way back up the creek. Well, I can tell you it was some climb, over rocks, through pools of water, up little waterfalls, and so on. In all that time we only caught one little trout, and Mundorff was the lucky rascal. It was so small, though, he put it in his back pocket, and I'll never forget when we were climbing up a little waterfall and Mundorff slipped and sat down on the little trout.

We made it to the top again about 4:00 p.m., dead tired and really ready for bed, or rather the pallet. Jack had brought along biscuits and a little meat, so we made our supper and turned in. The next morning we were up bright and early to catch the car down the mountain.

At the little station we ran into the mountaineer we had passed coming up. We were surprised to learn he had walked the entire

19 miles up the mountain and located his cattle. We made our way down the mountain about 10:30 or 11:00, and when we rounded a curve, there, stretched out across the track, were 10 or 12 men in khaki clothes and boots with pistols strapped on their sides.

They said they had to have the car, that they would return it later. Well, there was nothing else to do but let them have it, so we got off and sat down on the side of the tracks. The mountaineer came by and told us the men were revenue officers looking for Snuffy Smith's stills.

The mountaineer somehow or another had picked up through the grapevine that they were going to make this search, so he walked all night to put the word out. When the "revenooers" arrived the stills had disappeared and so had the whiskey makers.

In a couple of hours we heard the car coming around the curve. We all hopped in and finally got back down.

Well, it was a good thing that Jack came to Tech, because after that adventure I would have shot him myself had he not come. Dr. Sparks did his part while we were suffering the likes of the proverbial snowball, so all's well that ends well.

Punky Mundorff
(Better Known as Muddledorff)

Our little booklet would not be complete without our mentioning one of the great characters of our campus, who coached the only team that ever won the Southeastern Conference Basketball Championship and whose teams were contenders for many years. Roy Mundorff was more or less a jack of all trades, an outstanding math professor, basketball coach, baseball coach, naval officer, big operator, you name it.

I will never forget while I was stationed here at Tech during the war as executive officer of the Naval ROTC unit; we were playing our basketball games then in the old Naval Armory, which had seats for about 1200 people—about half on the court. Roy, who was also assigned to duty with that outfit, came to me and said "you know, I just bought a new car yesterday; since the papers say it is going down to about twelve tonight, how about driving it in the Armory overnight. I promise you I will have it out by ten."

Well, being an old sucker, I said sure, even though I knew Alex would be walking through there that morning and I didn't want him to find the car sitting on the basketball court. Roy's being in the Navy meant nothing to Alex, and I knew if he found a car there he would be after me. Nine o'clock rolled around and the car was still there. Ten o'clock came and the car was still there. Ten-thirty rolled around.

Alex came to my office and closed the door—Mundorff was standing in the corner—and the old man lit into me. You could hear him all over the place. Finally the bawling-out was over, and I opened the door and walked out with Mundorff right behind me. He stopped me and whispered "buddy, I should have said something but I didn't have the nerve."

There was a rather prominent Atlanta businessman also standing there, and he told me he wanted to see about getting his son into the Navy. He said "I wouldn't take that bawling out from anyone. You are a Lieutenant Commander in the Navy and you shouldn't put up with such things as that." I said "well you go in and tell the old man yourself, I ain't got the heart."

Mundorff was a great driver; everywhere he went he used a car. How he did it I don't know but he would also squeeze the last drop out of the tank and at times, in the early hours of the morning, he would run out of gas. But somehow or another he would get back on time, even if it was necessary to wake the filling station owner up. One night he hit a truckload of watermelons and spread them all over Upson county. Boy he could fly; 'way back there he drove from Atlanta to Albany in three hours, and when our wives (Mrs. Ector and Mrs. Griffin) heard about it we both received a dressing-down for riding with Punky and orders not to make a trip with him again.

Roy had one rather interesting experience, which only a few know about and I think worth mentioning. Soon after the lecture by W. A. Alexander, Roy was ordered by the Navy department to Harvard University where he was to become executive officer of the Naval ROTC and the Electronics School. Roy made friends easily, and found a friend on the faculty at Harvard, a guy who was working on the first computer in the country. Roy used to go down and watch him work. The machine was spread out all over the basement of one of the old buildings at Harvard, and being a mathematician himself, Roy became interested in what was being done.

Soon afterwards his friend decided he would join the Navy, which he did, receiving his commission and orders to report to a line officers school, which meant the end of the work on the computer. Roy, realizing the importance of the computer work, was quite concerned and wrote the Bureau of Personnel about the matter, but nothing was done about changing the orders. Roy finally got on the train, went down to the Bureau in Washington, and talked to them about what the new officer was doing. Realizing the importance of the work, the orders were changed and the work continued. If Roy were still alive, I'm afraid he would wonder if he did the right thing.

When you listen to the ladies when they receive their bills from the department store at times, it seems as if someone is always punching the wrong key.

The Shades of the Thirties

With another stock market debacle on us (right now there is a loss of $100,000,000,000 in paper profits) it brings the Thirties to mind to those of us who lived through the depression days. What a difficult time people had during those days. In fact, in some respects it was worse than a war. Millions of people lost their entire fortune, many hundreds committed suicide, and thousands of businesses failed. The total loss has never been estimated.

I can well remember when we were building the old Naval Armory and I saw a very nice looking old gentleman digging a ditch on the site. He was at least seventy years of age. I finally made friends with him, and spent a good deal of time talking to him.

He had at one time owned the Atlanta Baseball Club as one of his investments, but the only job he could get now was as a laborer with the WPA. But even with all of this there were a lot of funny things happening. When you look back upon them you just wonder.

One started about like this. One day the telephone rang and it was Alex asking me to come down to visit. Well, usually that meant trouble, so I took my time about getting there because I was sure there was a bawling out in the air. Instead, when I walked in he told me to have a seat instead of giving his usual greeting, "what the hell have you been doing now?"

I sat down and he said he wanted me to go out to the Veterans Administration with him to cash in his bonus (after World War I every veteran was given a bonus, and his amounted to $2,000). I had already cashed mine, so I asked if he really wanted to do that. He said he had to, that he hadn't drawn a salary for over nine months and he had to have something to live on. The Athletic Association had been paying him off in notes. There he was, head coach of a great institution's football team, and not drawing a cent of salary. What other coach would have done this?

Well, we went out and he cashed in his bonus and was able to hang on until the AA was able to start paying him again. They later took up all of his notes.

We only had two other full-time coaches at the time, Roy Mundorff and myself. Alex arranged for us to draw $200 a month since we were married and had children; otherwise, I don't know what we would have done. I remember when Armstrong called me in—I thought they were going to have to let me go—and I heaved a great sigh of relief and said a prayer when he said he was going to have to reduce my salary to $200 a month (I had been making $300). This was a great Godsend. Like Alex, they gave me notes for the rest, which I collected on later.

About a year later, my phone was ringing and it was Alex. Again, he said he wanted to see me. Well, the same feelings ran through me, but I made my way down to his office. Again I was received in a kindly manner, and he said "George, we have the football team coming in here the first of September and the Athletic Association doesn't have a dime. I have tried everything in the world to raise $5,000 because this is what it will cost us for the month. We have no money and the banks will not lend the Athletic Association a penny. I just can't see what we can do."

We talked on and on and I thought of one more chance, the Morris Plan Bank. This was a poor man's bank founded to help people in the lower-income group. We talked to Bob Schilling, an old Tech boy, who was the vice president. (By the way, the Morris Plan Bank is now the great National Bank of Georgia.)

Bob asked us to be seated and, with crocodile tears rolling down our cheeks, we told our story. It must have had its effect because Bob began to show interest, and when he really found out that it would have a great effect on the Georgia Tech football team, his *Alma Mater,* he began to loosen up.

Well, after lots of talk and palavering, he decided he would lend me $5,000 since I was employed and making $200 a month. Alex endorsed the note, and there was Bob with a note for $5,000 signed by a man earning $200 a month and endorsed by another who was not making anything. What a deal.

Naturally, before he agreed to the loan we made all kinds of promises. The main one was that we would surely repay him in some manner some day. In fact, we told him we would really do him a big favor as soon as we could. Well, we picked up the check and rushed out to the office to tell Mrs. Williamson to write the boys to report on September first as usual. Then we added, now you must pay this back at $550 per month or thereabouts.

Mrs. Williamson's face fell, but by golly she paid it back within a year so we were home free.

I will never forget many years later, just before the Georgia game, I went down and tried to chisel her out of a couple of tickets. She said she didn't have even one ticket. I then told her that the AA was getting just like everyone else. Everyone is just a number and human relations mean nothing. I went on to say that I wished the good old days were here again and she looked at me with a twinkle in her eye and said "I don't want any more old times like they were when you and Coach Alex were running this business." She had never forgotten about the $5,000 she had to sweat out.

Naturally, it came time for the big favor we were going to do for Bob Schilling. Every year the phone would ring about the first of the year and Bob would ask where that big favor was. Well, this brought on a long explanation and every year we were able to stave him off, but old Bob was persistent. This went on for 28 years, I believe. You could look for the call a little after January 1 each year, asking the same question.

Well, Coach Alex died suddenly. Shortly afterward the Alumni decided to honor his memory by building the Alexander Memorial Building, and $1,500,000 was donated by the Alumni and Friends of the Institute; that's when the Athletic Board got us off the hook. They deposited the million and a half in Bob's bank and the load was lifted from our shoulders. The bank had the use of the money for three or four years.

I still tell this story on Bob. I told the officers in his bank about this transaction and they looked at him in horror. They never would have taken such a chance, but it did come home to roost.

The Fat Man's Revenge

The fall of 1919 was, as far as football was concerned, an up-and-down year. Tech had a great team on certain days and on others not so hot, losing one or two games they should have won hands down. There was some excuse, though, because many of the men were veterans; after a loss of a year or more on the field of play it took them a long time to return to playing form.

One game that we lost was to Washington and Lee, 3 to 0. Offhand I can't remember the Washington and Lee man who kicked the field goal that won the game, but I do remember the gloom that pervaded the campus after this defeat. I hate to say so but I always felt that Coach Heisman's attitude toward the game had a great deal to do with our defeat. I believe he later admitted that he was at fault because of the way he prepared for this game.

The following week we were to play Vanderbilt, an undefeated team with some of the greatest players in the South in her lineup such as Josh Cody, All-American tackle; Tom Lipscomb, All-Southern tackle; and others. During the entire week before the Washington and Lee game with the exception of a lecture or so, Washington and Lee was not mentioned. But the squad heard plenty about Vanderbilt, and the scrubs used Vanderbilt's plays against the Varsity for two weeks before the game. When Washington and Lee came around, the Techs were flat as a pancake and took a licking, the only time Washington and Lee defeated Tech.

Well, the day of the Vandy game rolled around. Tension was high and excitement ruled the roost, because we just had to redeem ourselves.

Fay Wood was our line coach and a prominent businessman in Atlanta as well. He was a great end from Notre Dame, and came out in the afternoons during the fall to coach the linemen.

The boys were dressing, and quiet prevailed throughout the room. Wood came in and walked up to Uncle Roy Huffines. Huff was about 5 feet 5, the original 5 by 5 man, weighed about 240 pounds and from time to time moved like molasses in the sunshine. As Fay walked up, Huff was bent over tying his shoe. Fay called Huffines a big fat tub of lard (or words to that effect) and said he had played the sorriest game at tackle the previous Saturday that he had ever seen. Huff jumped up mad and excited, with tears in his eyes, and told the coach he couldn't say that because he hadn't even played the last Saturday.

That didn't faze Coach Wood. He slammed Roy back down on the bench and told him if he had played he would have played a rotten game.

Well, that was too much. Huff didn't have an answer. The team filed out and the game started. Alex started Huff, who by that time was really steamed up. Afterwards Alex said he never saw a fat man play such a game.

It was a funny game. As far as I can remember, we couldn't do a thing. Tech made, I believe, only one first down, but that was when Buck Flowers was beginning to come into his prime. Tech beat Vandy 19 to 0; Flowers ran two kicks back for touchdowns and, if I am not mistaken, made a long run for the other. On Buck's last punt return, there was only one man between him and the goal. Huff had been knocked down and was climbing to his feet when he saw the situation. With the speed of Barney Oldfield, Roy jumped up and cut the last man down.

Maybe Coach Wood's bawling out did the job.

Sportsmanlike Conduct

Several years ago Tech was playing Georgetown which, at that time, was one of the powers in the East.

Georgetown had a great All-American end on its team, a big lad by the name of Florence.

Al Staton was playing tackle that year. (He could play anywhere on the line and was one of the greatest linemen we ever had.)

Florence kept holding Al. Finally, Al told him if he didn't quit holding him he was going to knock him out. Well, Florence was not afraid of the devil himself so he continued to hold Al.

Tech had the ball on Georgetown's seven-yard line at the time, and Tech was ahead 21 to 0.

All of a sudden here came a headgear flying through the air and off the field and right behind came Albert on the run. About that time, Mike Thompson picked up the ball and started to penalize Tech half the distance to the goal line for slugging (that was the penalty along with disqualification at that time).

The teams started back up the field and there was old Florence, cold as a cucumber, lying stretched out with not a muscle moving and, in the meantime, Alex had asked me what had happened.

I told him I didn't know, but we soon found out. When Al reached the bench he told Alex what happened. Alex silently directed Al to go sit on the bench, and the game finally ended 28 to 0 in favor of Tech.

After the game Al came to me and asked me to do him a favor.

Wondering what it could be, I said I would. He went on to say that he was supposed to go to Newnan, Georgia that evening to speak to the Boy Scouts on good sportsmanship, but he felt that it would be carrying it too far after what had happened. I called and Al retired from circulation until Monday.

That Is How an Indian Smells

In 1916, when Tech had one of its greatest football teams and won the Southern Championship, a big banquet was held at the Druid Hills Golf Club. Among those present was George W. Adair, who was really the father of big-time football at Georgia Tech. Mr. Adair, an alumnus of Georgia Tech, was at that time the most prominent man in our city and practically lived Tech football.

Mr. Adair was standing in the lobby of the club talking to Charlie Wahoo, one of our assistant coaches, and standing alongside his father was Jack Adair, then a little tad of about seven. Like all youngsters you never know what they might say or do, so out of a clear sky Jack said to his Dad "Father, Mr. Wahoo has been drinking."

Well, this took Charlie back, but, quick as a flash, Charlie said "no son, that is just the way an Indian smells."

Note: Jack is one of our most prominent citizens, as President of the Adair Realty Company, which is now over 100 years old.

What is the Price of Peanuts?

One day Doctor Coon came in and spoke to one of our greatest football stars saying "Mr. Burdell, what is the price of peanuts today?" Mr. Burdell spoke up and said they were five cents a pack across the street at Pap Neri's. (Pap Neri's stood where the dining hall is now.) Dr. Coon reached in his pocket took out a nickel and told Burdell to go over and buy a pack of peanuts, since that was the only question he would answer correctly in that class all semester.

Tech's First Ringer

One day just about the time people started traveling by air and passing the railroads by, I was coming back from Birmingham, riding the Pullman (The AA was paying the bill.). It was pretty lonesome and I was the only person in the car at the time, when the Pullman conductor walked down the aisle. He was a big, fine-looking man of about six feet three, about 250 in weight, and about 60 or 65. He was about as lonesome as I was, so he sat down and we started talking. Finally he asked my business and I said I was connected with Georgia Tech. He said that was quite interesting, that he played tackle on the Tech football team for three years. I immediately pricked up my ears and said "what was your class?" He said "oh, I never did attend Tech, I was the janitor in Knowles dormitory and since no one objected to my playing, I spent three years on the team."

This is rather interesting because on the first team in 1892, Professor Frank Spain of the Math Department played fullback and coached the team. The rules were really lax in those days. One year in the early 1900's Georgia came over to play Tech. Georgia had not won for a year or so, so they were determined to win that year. They brought over a team of ringers, as the story goes, and fifty dollars was offered to any Georgia man who made a touchdown. Well, Georgia ran up and down the field, but every time they reached the Tech goal there was a big wrangle as to who would make the touchdown and they never scored. Tech won. This was a great scandal. The papers were full of it, and somewhere around here I have all the stories about the Georgia team giving the real names of the players and the names used in the game. Some day I am going to try to find this. It happened about 1907.

An Old One

For years we have all been bragging and boasting about just how well Tech instructs the youth of our nation. We always feel that Georgia Tech men measure up to any engineering school graduates in America, and to prove this statement we always tell the old story that follows (usually filling in the name of some Tech Civil Engineer who might be in the audience).

In Tifton, Georgia there is a nice old hotel by the name of the Myon. It has a rather fine reputation and is well known to the traveling men throughout Georgia. One day the train stopped in Tifton and two people got off. One was an elderly man with two bags, and the other was a young buck just out of college and on the way to a new job. The Myon Hotel is close to the railroad station, so both walked up to the hotel. As they walked in, the young man stood back to allow the old gent to register. The old gentleman registered as S. V. Sanford, A.B., M.A., Ph.D., Athens, Georgia. The bellboy picked up his bags and walked off with them followed by Dr. Sanford. The young fellow stepped up to the register, saw the name as described above and asked the clerk what in the world did "A.B., M.A., Ph.D." mean? The clerk said he must be pretty dumb. In the first place, he should know that gentleman since he was one of the best-known men in the state of Georgia. That was Dr. S. V. Sanford, Chancellor of the University System of Georgia. That "A.B." meant that he had attended college four years with honor and they gave him a degree called a Bachelor of Arts. The "M.A." meant that he had continued his education for one or two more years and upon the completion of his work, they gave him another degree known as a Master of Arts. The Ph.D. was the highest degree a man could earn, and he was now known as a Doctor of Philosophy.

The young man signed his name to the old-fashioned register as George P. Burdell, S.I. The clerk look at it and asked what the "S.I." meant. With that, the lad said he must be pretty dumb himself, because that meant that he was a graduate of Georgia Tech and held the degree of Civil Engineering.

Captain's Inspection

When Captain J. V. Babcock (Commanding Officer of Georgia Tech's NROTC) was Commandant of the Naval Reserve

Officer's Training Corps at Harvard University, during the time
that Dr. Elliott was President of Harvard, a rather interesting
occurance took place.

Dr. Elliott and Mrs. Elliott were preparing for a reception for
the faculty of the university, and on the date of the reception
Captain Babcock, who was naturally invited, walked in a little
early to pay his respects to Mrs. Elliott before the arrival of
the guests.

During the conversation Mrs. Elliott said that she had spent
the past two months cleaning the President's home from basement to attic. With this Captain Babcock asked if she was ready
for the Captain's Inspection. She said she was, so the Captain, who
was wearing white gloves, walked over to the door that led to
the drawing room, ran his fingers across the top, and held out
his hand to show it to Mrs. Elliott.

It was three months before Mrs. Elliott spoke to him again.

One of the great problems of the Memphis Class Cruisers was
keeping the washroom clean. During the year the Admiral in
command made his annual inspection, which was a pain in the
neck to the commanding officers. He immediately went to the
wash room when he arrived on board. Naturally they could never
meet the high standards of the Navy Department, but Captain
Babcock was determined that the next annual inspection would
be conquered and they would hit the old man in the eye.

When the day arrived, the Admiral headed for the wash
room as usual. He looked it over and was thoroughly astounded.
He turned to the Seaman Guard and asked how he did it. The
Seaman said "sir, we haven't allowed anyone in here for three
days!"

Bob Jones in Pud's Drawing Class

All you old-timers remember Pud Lowndes and some of his
sayings; well, one time the backlash caught him.

Bob Jones was in drawing class when Pud came by. Bob was
trying to lift one of the thumbtacks with the edge of his triangle,

and if you remember, triangles in those days had a little indention in the sides to help pick them up. Pud looked down and in his loud voice said "you'll never be an engineer; why don't you use your watch? That triangle is of more value than your watch." He scared old Bob to death.

Well the next week rolled around, and Pud was on his usual prowl around the class when all of a sudden he was stopped in his tracks. One of his students sitting close to Bob was banging on his thumbtack with his watch. "Stop," cried Pud, "you'll ruin that watch." The lad looked up and said "Professor, you told Mr. Jones to use his watch to remove his thumbtacks and I am just following your orders." Pud looked so pitiful that the lad admitted that it was just a dollar watch and that they had taken the works out and filled it with concrete just to have some fun with him. Pud laid off that line for a long time.

The World's Greatest Salesman

A few years ago Tobe Edwards, who was a member of the football squad and one of our greatest, was coaching the Milligan College football team in the fall and playing first base for Tampa in the South Atlantic League. Tampa had a right good team that year and made the play-off. Of course the play-off came after the regular season, which meant that Tobe had to hang around three or four extra days after the close of the season to take part. He called the President of Milligan explaining his situation and asking permission to miss the first three days of football practice. Permission was granted and Tobe stayed over. As soon as the last game was over his bags had been packed and he left the field in a cloud of dust for Milligan. Flying through Lakeland the speed cop spotted him and finally chased him down. Then the salesmanship started. Tobe went to explaining his position, asking for mercy and asking permission to continue with his trip, but to no avail. Tobe then took a good look at the policeman and saw he was a young man in his early twenties, six feet one or two inches tall and weighing about two-twenty.

A great idea struck friend Tobe. He began talking football to the young officer and soon found out he had played on the local high school team as a tackle. Tobe then really buckled down. He gave him all the arguments as to the value of a college education, all the pretty girls he would meet. the good times he would have as a college student and ended up offering him a scholarship. Finally the bait worked. The young man grabbed it hook, line and sinker. He drove into a filling station, parked his motorcycle, took off his cap, unstrapped his gun, hung it on the handle bars, walked into the station and called the chief of police to tell him he was resigning and that he was leaving his motorcycle at a certain filling station along with his cap and gun. Then he jumped into Tobe's car and off they went for Milligan where he played tackle four years, received his degree and went back out into the world with a degree and the hope he would make that money Tobe had told him about.

The Visit to Snooky Woods

One day during Spring football practice, Ralph McGill, then sports editor of *The Atlanta Constitution,* came by the dressing room. It was raining cats and dogs when McGill came in, and Alex was sitting there talking to Hal Voorhees who was then general manager of A. G. Spalding for this district. I was track coach at the time and we were going ahead with practice under the stadium, so I had a ringside seat.

Finally McGill said "well, you can't have football practice today and I have three tickets to the Atlanta Theater to see Snooky Woods so let's go down." (Snooky was a stripper, appearing at the Atlanta Theater.) Alex said he couldn't go and Voorhees said he had to take his wife to a tea at four o'clock. Well, McGill started pleading and Alex weakened under the strain and said he would go. Voorhees was still holding out, but with two of them on his back, he finally gave in. He called his wife and told her how sorry he was but the traveling auditor from Spalding's had just come to town and wanted to go over some tax matters.

With that they were off to see Snooky. Well, that was hunky dory and nothing was said about the matter. They even visited Snooky backstage after the show.

Next morning the fat was in the fire. Alex—this being before he was married—walked into the dining room, and found his mother reading *The Constitution*. Mrs. Alexander was a former school mistress, and giving Alex that old eagle eye asked "William, who is this Snooky Woods?" Alex looked over her shoulder at the paper, which was turned to the sports page, and his eyes glazed. McGill had written a two-column story covering a fourth of the first sports page about the men's visit to Snooky Woods.

Alex grumbled something, swallowed a cup of hot coffee and beat it out of there as soon as he could. He arrived at his office and the phone was ringing. He picked it up and there was Voorhees on the other end asking Alex to come out to his house at once. His wife was saying she was going to divorce him. Well, after two or three days things became normal again, but you could never get Alex or Hal Voorhees to ever go near the Atlanta Theater again.

Copy of a Letter to a New Student

Mr. Roddy Garrison,
Richmond, Va.

My dear Sir:

Some time ago we received from you a request for a catalog of the Georgia School of Technology, and I am writing to ask if there is any further information about the departments and the advantages of this institution which we can furnish you.

You probably know something of the value of a course in a technical school of high standard and of national reputation, where young men are educated for real efficiency. There is no other kind of higher training today which offers anything like the same opportunities for a successful career in a life work which is as attractive and remunerative as it is useful. The big industries of the world, those which are developing our natural resources and giving us the benefits of modern improvements in transportation, in power development, in structural work, in manufacturing, etc., are demanding each year more men who have been trained to think scientifically and to work efficiently.

The Georgia School of Technology has a reputation which is based on the real test of any institution, the success of its graduates. All of the alumni of the School are comparatively young men— 75% of them are under 35 years of age—and yet among their number may be found 12 Presidents of industrial corporations, 10 Vice Presidents, 28 General Managers, 24 Superintendents, 13 City Superintendents of Public Works, and hundreds of successful engineers in various fields.

The demand for Georgia Tech graduates was never greater than at present. There was not a man in the recent graduating class of 93 students who did not have a position offered to him before graduation, and many of them had the choice of several desirable positions. Representatives of the biggest corporations in America come to Georgia Tech to offer positions to members of the senior class.

Trusting that you received our catalog promptly, and hoping that we may have the pleasure of hearing from you in the near future.

Very truly yours,
K. G. Matheson
President

Things don't change much. Back in 1916 the President seems to have been an advertising man.

Professor Alexander

For several years after graduation from Tech Alex acted as an instructor in the math department. When he first started out he had his troubles. In the old days the school was so poor that the texts issued the professors had to be returned to the head of the department at the end of the year and since Alex was working for BoCat it had to go back. It was also true that you were not sure that you would get the same text back that you had used the year before. One of the professors was issued Alex's old book and every now and then he would find a problem with a circle around it and a note saying "don't fool with this one."

One day just before final exams one of his students told Alex he had to pass his exam or he would be fired from school. It was

(Continued on page 65.)

Lieutenant (later General) Leonard Wood, bottom right, was Tech's first "ringer." Frank Spain, fourth from left on back row, was also on the 1893 team that was rocked out of Athens after defeating Georgia's championship team.

Tech's 1915 Scrub team—George Griffin is third from right on front row; Dave "Dummy" LeBey on left end of front row; Coach Alexander standing on far left of back row.

Tech's 1916 Southern Champions, who won over Cumberland 222-0. "Canty" Alexander (far left, third row), after playing four years without a touchdown, finally made one against Cumberland.

The "Golden Tornado" of 1917, Coach Heisman's greatest team.

This 1920 squad was Tech's first freshman team, although a few transfer students played.

The 1920 version of Tech's "Golden Tornado" under Coach Alexander is considered by many to have been the school's greatest team even though they lost 10-3 to national champion Pittsburgh. Front row: George Ratterman, Al Staton, Oscar Davis, Amis, Dave (Dummy) LeBey, Bill Fincher, and John Staton. Back row: Jack McDonough, Red Barron, Judy Harlan, and Buck Flowers (captain).

The 1928 National Champions, one of Alexander's greatest teams—said by many to be Tech's most powerful.

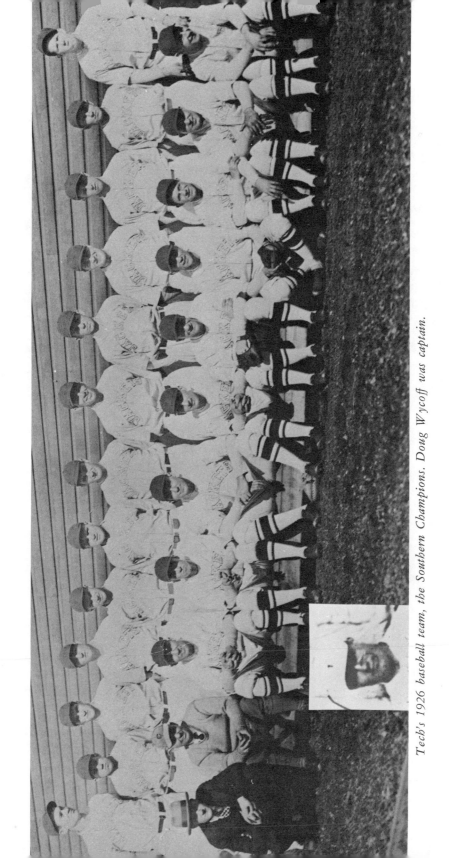

Tech's 1926 baseball team, the Southern Champions. Doug Wycoff was captain.

The only Tech basketball team to win the Southeastern Conference championship—1936
Roy Mundorff was coach.

Tech's 1936 Southeastern Conference cross-country championship team. Three later gave
their lives in World War II. Left to right: Joe Byrd, Eddie Fambrough (killed D-Day),
Johnson, Batson, Kestler (killed in the Battle of the Bulge), Jack Pearce, Chick Aldridge
(killed in China), Jim O'Callagan, Mills, and Goldman.

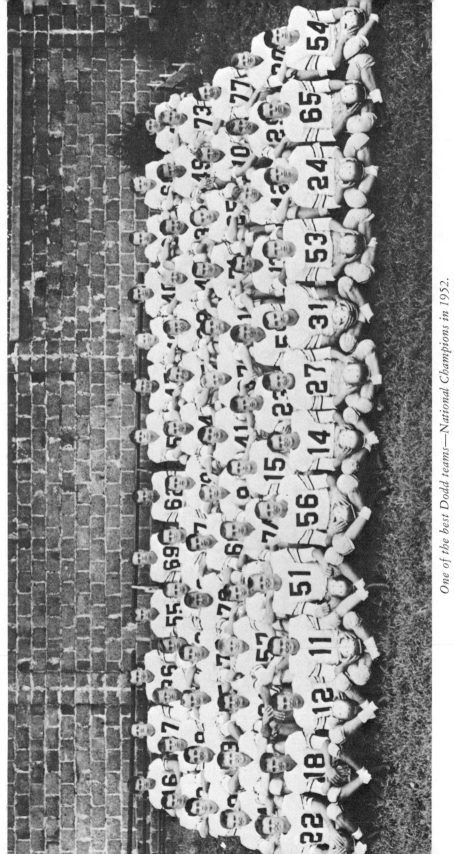

One of the best Dodd teams—National Champions in 1952.

Georgia Tech's 1957 Southeastern Conference Championship Baseball Team.

The Georgia Tech Tennis Team of 1960, Southeastern Conference Champions, with Coach/Professor Bortell.

during prohibition days and everyone was drinking Georgia corn, so in a kidding way Alex said "you get yourself an ice cream soda glass, fill it with Georgia corn, and in a few minutes your mind will work like an adding machine. You can't miss." Well, the day of the exam rolled around and the lad took one look, wrote his name on his Blue Book, tucked the exam inside, turned it in, and walked out. Alex was not pleased at all, but said nothing. That afternoon he saw the lad on the campus and asked him why he turned in a blank Blue Book. The lad said "Coach, after following your instructions I didn't give a damn whether I took the exam or not."

The Weight of the World

The name Burdell covers lots of sins, so here goes. You know D.M., at least most of the old timers do. One day one of the lads finally got his hair up (I guess you would now call him a dissenter) and objected to Dr. Smith about his supposed favoritism to some of his athletes. The complaint was about as follows: Dr. Smith was always doing something for the athletes. Why didn't he do something for the other boys in the class? They paid their own tuition and deserved the same treatment. D.M. said he was giving a big test on Monday which would count as a third of their monthly grade. He said he would improve their grade by doubling their average or mark, then multiplying this total by two. This would be their grade for the month. It was agreed upon. Wednesday the grades were read out, and finally Mr. Burdell's name came to the fore. Dr. Smith told Mr. Burdell his grade on the test was zero. Now if he doubled this, the result was still zero, then he multiplied this by two and the result was still zero. Therefore his test grade was zero. This was the end of the discussion.

Another time one of the many Mr. Burdells on the campus was assigned a homework problem in calculus to determine the weight of the world. After an all-night struggle the paper was complete, and when handed in to Dr. Smith the next day it was discovered that Mr. Burdell had calculated that the world weighed the tremendous total of six tons. D.M. kept telling this story, always giving the lad's name. Finally one day Mr. Burdell came out to see Dr. Smith and said he wanted him to quit telling that story about the weight of the world. He was in the insurance business, and after giving the prospect his name as they sat down for a serious discussion of his problem, the prospect always interrupted to ask if he wasn't the fellow who calculated the weight of the earth as six tons and there went his sale out the window.

Nothing Ever Happens in Atlanta
The Most Famous Bear That Ever Lived

Right after the Rose Bowl game of 1929, Chip Robert was presented a little bear cub by the California friends of Georgia Tech. Chip did not know what to do with a little bear so he gave it to Stumpy Thomason. Well, Stumpy was rather nonplussed for a while but kept the little rascal, and between keeping him in his room and under the East Stands the bear survived and became a great favorite of all the students.

In fact, they taught him all kinds of tricks. They taught him to drink Coca-Cola and, like all bad boys, taught him to hit the bottle, so he had to have his nip now and then. On some of the football trips he was borrowed by the Alumni, rode in the baggage car and, I am sorry to say, at times he became looping drunk. One day coming back from a trip to Florida he was brought through the dining car and nothing would suit him except to sweep all the dishes off the tables.

I will never forget Vance Maree who was rooming with Stumpy in that famous dormitory they had on Luckie Street across from Dr. Cox's drug store. (What a tale that old building could tell.) Vance finally told Stumpy he was going to move out because he couldn't take it any longer. By that time the bear had grown to weigh about 150 pounds. Vance and Stumpy were sleeping on double deckers and Stumpy had the lower bunk. The bear couldn't get in there so every night he would jump into bed with Vance, which made for a tussle as to who would have the cover and the room. Stumpy looked at Vance with a sad expression and said he hated to lose a good roommate but it would have to be. Well, all this leads up to Mike Chambers and his pal Lee Jensen.

Going over on the Olympic boat in the summer, Alex met Mike who was the trainer of the Olympic Swimming team that year. Alex was quite impressed with his work and after awhile offered Mike a job at Tech as trainer of all athletic teams. Mike accepted and arrangements were made for him to report.

The summer passed and football season drew nigh. Alex received a letter from Mike stating that he would arrive in Atlanta on August 31 about two p.m. and would drive down to the campus about four p.m. Alex wrote back and said he would be delighted to see him at Tech, he would leave the training room open in case he arrived earlier, and he would meet him there at four o'clock. Mike and Lee hurried along and arrived in Atlanta about two p.m., drove out to Grant Field, and sat around waiting on Alex. As all of you know, if there is a lonesome place in the world on Sunday it is a football stadium. Mike and Lee sat there for an hour or so and finally Mike turned to Lee and said they had made the biggest mistake of their lives by accepting this job because nothing had happened here since 1865 when Sherman marched through Atlanta. He hadn't finished the sentence when in walked a big 300 pound bear. Mike and Lee froze. Their next thought was what to do to get away from such a terrible monster. All of you oldsters remember how small the training room was. There was a large packing case in one corner where Burton and Porto had been unpacking some gear and Lee, being a slim, alert six footer, made for the packing case, turned it over, and got under it. Mike started running around and finally saw a little door with a spool nailed on it for a knob. This was where Porto and Burton kept their turpentine and other rubbing supplies. Mike managed to squeeze into this, got the door closed and there he was. It was hot as the dickens. No ventilation or air-conditioning at the time, and Mike and Lee were in for it. The bear would go up to the door of the cabinet, bang on the door, then go over to the packing case where he would scratch around for action from the inside. This went on for thirty or forty minutes. Finally Alex walked in, ran the bear out and started looking around. He heard a little voice coming from the box, crying for help. Alex turned the box over and there was Lee, covered with perspiration and dust. Then they started looking for Mike. Alex pulled the little door open and out fell Mike. He landed on the floor and passed out. Alex ran and got a bucket of cold water and poured it over Mike. Mike finally came to, looked up at Alex, and said he would never say that nothing ever happened in Atlanta again.

The answer to the excitement was that the boys had taught the bear to take a shower each day, and since it was Sunday and no one was around he finally shook off his chain and wandered into the dressing room looking for someone to turn on his shower. That bear really created lots of excitement.

You Can't Pass Anyhow

Old Herr Doc (Doctor Crenshaw, who was head of the Modern Language department for many years) was a real character and lots of fun. As he became older, if you could recite and shoot him (as the fellows used to say in those days) he would give you an A. If you were absent from class he would also mark an A in his roll book. The only thing was that both A's looked just alike. So when he went to make up the exemption list for the final exam, nearly everyone was exempt. During the last two weeks he hardly had a corporal's guard in class.

He really ran his department. He did just as he pleased. Sometimes if you failed the first semester, he would say that if you passed the second semester he would give you credit for the first term's work. Sometimes he would forget, then there was a long argument with his lads. But if he said you had to take the first term exam over, you took it. I know because this happened to me. By the end of the second semester you had forgotten what you had been over during the first semester, and I am telling you, it was hard to pass the exam under those circumstances. Sometimes he would only give you a day's notice.

Well, anyhow, George P. Burdell, one of our great football stars (I would tell you his name but he told me if he caught me telling this story on him again he was going to give me a good licking) went by class before the exam one day and asked Doc to give an old exam to study, since he had to pass Spanish to be eligible the next year. Doc, whose desk looked like W. C. Field's, picked up the first paper he saw and handed it to George. George took it down to his room and for a week every time you passed his door, he would be lying on his sack trying to memorize *Señor* and so on. Finally, the exam rolled around and George reported as ordered. The exams were passed out and as George looked at it, he recognized some of the words and took action at once. George may have been the poorest student in the class but he was honest as the days were long and a man of high ideals, as he has proven throughout his long life. He walked up to the front of the class and Doc asked what he wanted. George said he couldn't take the exam, Doc asked why, and George said it was the same exam Doc had given him to study. Doc said go and take it, since he couldn't pass it anyhow. George did and he made a thirty-five.

Another short story about George: There was an old rule at the time that if a professor was late over 15 minutes, the students could leave the class without penalty. Well, one day, thirteen minutes had passed when some big lad got up and said to go. Well, most of the class got up and started out. The big boy noticed George sitting still and walked over and said to go, and called George chicken. George rose up and said he was studying and with that he knocked our big friend down. Well, all the others who were so ready to leave came back, sat down, and waited until a minute or so longer than the legal time had passed before they left. That guy Burdell was quite a man.

Sort of a Young One Ain't He?

This story has many variations, so you will have to pardon us for repeating it. It happened to Coach Alexander in San Francisco shortly before his death.

As we all know Tech had an arrangement with the University of California, entered into right after the Rose Bowl game of 1929. The contract read that once during every college generation or once every four years Tech would visit Berkeley for a post season game and the University of California was to visit Tech once during this same period. On this particular trip the Press Club gave a dinner in San Francisco in honor of Coach Alexander and the Tech party.

After the Tech team arrived in San Francisco and disembarked from the ferry, which was operating at that time, they were met by the President of the Chamber of Commerce and other distinguished citizens of the city. They were placed in cars and taken on a sight seeing trip. One of the sights visited was the famous Golden Gate Bridge. After a thorough inspection of this great structure, one of the hosts made a little preliminary speech in which he described the Golden Gate as the greatest bridge ever built by man, adding there was none other like it in existence. Then he asked Alex what he thought of the bridge. Alex looked around and said, "Well it's OK, but there are four just like it across Peachtree Creek in Atlanta." (Alex of course was just ribbing his host, since he knew Californians always thought anything they had was the greatest in the world.) He was overheard by one of the California group, who made up his mind then and there that he would get even with that Georgia Cracker. The party left the bridge to visit the other sights of this great city, but the gentleman in question left and went by Fisherman's Wharf where he had delivered to Alex's room a big sea turtle weighing about 399 pounds. (He knew that several members of the group were coming back to Alex's room for a highball or so and a little football talk.) The party returned and were sitting around shooting the breeze when the gentleman in question spoke up and said "Alex, have you ever seen a California bed bug?" Alex said no, and with that the gentleman got up, walked over to the bed, threw back the covers, and there was the big turtle. Here, he said, is a fair representative of our bed bugs. Well, this didn't faze Alex at all. He took one look, turned around, and said "he's sort of a young one ain't he?"

Canty and Quack Jackson

O f course it is an old story about heating up a thermometer, but Canty Alexander really trapped Quack Jackson one day. Dr. Jackson was our school physician and had been for many years. He was also the doctor for the football team and knew all the boys real well, in fact everyone called him "Quack." Well, Canty was too lazy to go to class one day so he decided to go by the hospital and see what he could do with Quack and, if possible, get an excuse to miss class. He dropped into the clinic, or rather the little room Quack had set aside to interview the boys. When he asked Canty what was wrong, Canty said he was feeling bad and would like to turn in. Quack stuck a thermometer in his mouth and walked out into the ward for a minute. After a few minutes he came back. In the meantime Canty had placed the thermometer on the radiator. When he heard Quack on the way back he stuck it in his mouth. Quack came in, grabbed it out of his mouth, looked at it and started screaming, "Nurse, Nurse, get a bed, he is burning up." The thermometer read 108 degrees. Canty was immediately hustled to a bed, given all attention possible and managed to miss his class.

Canty was always up to something. I remember after World War I Canty had gone to work for a textile company in North Charleston, South Carolina. I was working in Charleston that summer with the Standard Oil Company of New Jersey and one day he called me up and asked if I'd come out Sunday and spend the day with him. I agreed and the following Sunday reported to Canty's residence. The only place Canty could find to live was with the minister of a little Presbyterian church. Well, soon after Canty moved in the minister went to work on him. The first thing I did when I checked in was go to Sunday School where Canty taught a class. After this he went upstairs to open up the church and make things ready for the church services. He took up the collection, and after the service closed up the church. On the way back to his house I started kidding him in a friendly fashion and told him he must be a deacon in the church. He said yes, but he was getting damn tired of it.

After a good many years Canty found a wonderful girl ready to put up with his foolishness. One day Strupper and I were on a trip through South Carolina for the school and ran out of money. We were in Greenville at the time so we went down to the bank and gave the man our story. He took a chance and let us have five or ten dollars to get back to Atlanta. Leaving the bank, who would turn up but Canty. We began to talk to him and after awhile he started telling us about his married life and how he was the boss in his household. About that time a lady came through the front door of the bank. Canty looked up and said it was Mrs. Alexander. Now, Strup quick as a flash started on the dead run for her. The bank was crowded with people and Canty burst out in his stentorian voice "don't believe that fellow, he is the biggest liar in Georgia." Well, the banking business came to a stop until the situation was cleared up.

Canty was of the most peculiar build. He used to say that his hose supporters slipped up instead of down. Our modern youth probably never saw a pair of old-fashioned hose supporters.

Just before the Georgia game in 1916 Tech started to Athens for the game on the Seaboard train. On the way over Canty went to Coach Heisman and told him he thought the fellows were overconfident and he wanted to make a speech to the team before they got there. Well, we were staying at the old Georgian Hotel in Athens. We were so afraid that those rascals would do something to us that we carried our own water over plus our own food, which we ate just before the game. Finally Coach Heisman ran all the squad members out except those who were to start the game, and knowing that most of us were not going to play we immediately began to stuff ourselves.

Later we heard about Canty's speech. Canty got up and said

words to this effect: "come on, you big fat stiffs, let's go out and knock the stuffing out of those guys." Then he sat down. Everyone came out looking very grim. The game was played and Tech ran all over the Bulldogs, Tommy Spence being the star of the game. In fact, Morgan Blake wrote a long poem about "How the Jackets Rode to Glory on the Back of Tommy Spence." Strupper was supposed to run wide and they were set for him, so Johnny rigged up a few plays hiding the ball and handing off to Spence.

After the game Tally Johnston went to Canty, and said he wanted him to know that the fellows resented what he said in his speech because they did not like to be called rather obnoxious names. Canty was terribly shocked about what Tally had said, and answered by saying he didn't say that. Finally it all came out. In his excitement he had mixed up his words, so all was well. I wish I could really tell you what he said but such words are not used in polite company by Tech men.

The Story of the Majorettes

W hen Ben Sisk, our fine band leader, first came to Tech he did everything to rejuvenate the band. Since he had watched the majorettes while conducting one of the local high school bands in Atlanta he felt that if he could get permission to invite some of the high school girls to strut in front of Tech's band it would enliven the students and in general pep things up. Along with Walter Herbert, director of the Glee Club and head of the little music department here at Tech, they prepared a paper extolling the advantages of majorettes and away they went to read it to Alex. Alex told the gentlemen to have a seat and asked if they had a problem. Well, according to my story Walter was supposed to read the paper, but he hesitated so long that Ben finally took it over and started. The paper was a most glowing article showing all the advantages of the majorettes and after it was finished, everyone sat there for a minute and nothing was said. Finally Alex asked if that was all; Ben said "yes," and Alex then said "no women, period." After Alex died it was not long before we had majorettes, and it is a good thing we got them because Tech was soon co-ed and we had our own young ladies.

Look Homeward Dr. Perry

If you remember *Look Homeward Angel,* it should bring to mind to you old timers old Fred Wolfe, who graduated in 1922 in EE. He was the brother of the famous Thomas Wolfe, the writer. Tom went to the University of North Carolina where he began his writing and Fred came to Tech.

By the way, when the Drama-Tech club produced *Look Homeward Angel* they invited Fred and Mrs. Wolfe down from Spartanburg as their guests for a weekend and a look at their efforts with this great production. Fred said that Tech's was better than the Broadway show, which was quite a compliment.

This brings up what happened to Fred when he ran into difficulties with Dr. Perry, who was at that time chairman of the absence committee. I am sure you remember the old rule that any man having seven unexcused absences in any one quarter would be dropped from the rolls. (I remember Snooks Hoffman being dropped in the last half of the semester while a senior for this infraction.) Well, early in the first semester of Fred's sophomore year he overcut and Dr. Perry had him in. He came out with a frown on his face, mad as a wet hen. One of his fellow culprits asked Fred what happened. Fred said (he stuttered when he was angry), that old so-and-so stole my money and I am going to a g-oo-ood s-c-hoool, Carnegie Tech. Well, he didn't. He stayed out the rest of the year, but showed up the following fall and went on to graduate. Tom Wolfe wrote this up in a most inimitable style in his book, *Look Homeward Angel,* and after reading the book and seeing Dr. Perry on occasions when things were not going well, I would always say "Doctor, you had better watch out or Tom Wolfe will put you in another book." This would always bring a smile to his face because, when I look back over the situation, it was rather ridiculous.

Mind Your Own Damn Business

All of the ROTC boys as well as the boys in the Navy V5 and V12 programs remember Chief Fickes, Chief Signalman attached to the ROTC at that time. Old Fickes was quite a character. I remember one day Joe Pittard came in and asked Fickes where Roy Mundorff was. Fickes said he didn't know but he could tell him what he was doing. Joe asked what was he doing. Fickes said he was counting his money. Joe came in my office and sug-guested we find Roy. We started on a search and when we finally found Roy, sure enough, he was counting money. It was not his, but if he had one nickel on the desk, there must have been three or four thousand. Roy was welfare officer for the ROTC and had just cleared the Coke machines. Cokes were only a nickel then as you may remember.

Anyhow, before reporting to Tech, Fickes had been Chief Signalman on the\ USS Lexington. The Captain at the time was Admiral Ernie King, later Commander-in-Chief of our naval forces during World War II. Captain King had the reputation in the Navy of being a sundowner. Anyhow, Fickes and his pal the Chief Quartermaster had the watch. This was just before World War II started, and the Lexington was on a practice maneuver, running about thirty knots with all lights out on a mission to a port in Cuba. Fickes and his friend were standing in the wing of the bridge, port side, when they passed a big liner. The ship was all lit up, the band was playing, and the young cruise people were dancing and having a high old time. About that time Fickes heard a noise behind him and looked up. There was Captain King. Fickes was standing on one side of the pelorus (used for taking bearings), and his friend was on the other. His friend had not heard the Captain. Fickes eased out of the way so the old man could take a look. About that time, his pal asked if he knew what he would like to be doing. There was no answer, so he went ahead. He would sure like to be over there with a highball in one hand and a good looking blonde by the other and going to town. This was too much for the Skipper. He looked over at the Quartermaster and told him to keep his mind on his damn business.

Not Until I Get Up There

At sea either in the Navy or in the Merchant Marine, the Captain of a ship is king, at least in his small world. Well, in our Navy, on one of the old battleships, there was such a commanding officer. He had to be in everything. On every Navy ship, church services are held every Sunday. This Captain would always come, but he was always late. One Sunday the old Padre was ready to start the service, but no Captain. According to Hoyle he couldn't start until the Skipper arrived, so he waited and waited. The men were beginning to get restless and the time allotted for the service was passing rapidly. Finally, in desperation, the chaplain decided to go ahead. Being an Episcopalian, he started his service, as is customary in that church, with a preparatory sentence and said "the Lord is in his Holy Temple." With that the Skipper, whose cabin was directly under the quarterdeck where the service was being held, dragged a chain under the hatch right in the middle of the quarterdeck and said "not until I get up there."

Always Clack Ice

In the old Navy the government had gunboats stationed on the Yangtze River. One of Tech's good friends tells this story about Captain Mark C. Bowman, former Commanding Officer of the Tech ROTC Unit.

While a midshipman (In the old days after graduation from the Naval Academy everyone had to serve one year as a midshipman before being commissioned an ensign.), he was stationed on one of the old gunboats making its way up and down the river. In those days the Navy hired Chinese natives who became the mess boys and remained on the ships sometimes as long as twenty-five to thirty years. Of course in time they really owned the ship. The Captain was just a figurehead.

The young officers were sitting around the wardroom one day, shooting the breeze and sipping highballs. Navy ships carried Wine Messes at that time. It was only after Josephus Daniels became Secretary of the Navy that they were discontinued. After awhile, one of the young lads spoke to the old Chinese mess boy, who was over in the corner of the wardroom at the sink near the galley cracking ice. He asked him "since you are my mess boy, why don't you ever shine my shoes?" Another officer spoke up and said "you are my mess boy, too, why don't you clean up my bunkroom?" With that, the old rascal turned around and said "no time to shine shoes. Always clack ice."

Anchors Away

Having spent several years in the Navy it is natural to pick up a few stories that might be of interest to many of our Alumni who have spent time during World War I, World War II, the Korean War and in Vietnam. So forgive an old story teller.

It seems that one day Captain J. V. Babcock, USN (who by the way was Commanding Officer of the Naval Unit here at Tech for two or three years during the late war) was bringing the Medusa, one of the great repair ships of the Navy, into San Diego harbor. As luck would have it the Pacific Fleet was in, and of course the battleships, cruisers and destroyers had all the buoys locked up as well as the prize places alongside the docks. The skipper and his executive officer were really up against it as to where they would tie up the Medusa. Finally they spied an old dock some distance away. Making way to the top they managed to see why no one wanted to tie up there. The roofs had fallen in on the warehouses, the cross-ties had fallen through the rotted-out dock, and in general it was no place to tie up a big ship. A young seaman was sent ashore to handle the lines, the Medusa was brought alongside, and number one line was passed ashore. The youngster looked around and found not a bollard in sight. As a last resort, he took a turn around the rails running beside the warehouse. This upset the old Bo'sun terribly so in his best stentorian voice he yelled "belay that, it won't hold." This didn't phase the lad, who yelled back "the hell it won't, the other end is in St. Louis."

The Great Safari

Prior to World War II, Mitchell Cox, now Vice-President of the Pepsi Cola Company, was a professor in the English department. One of Mitchell's jobs was to teach public speaking (He was a fine speaker himself.). It is useless to remind you fellows about how difficult it was to find someone adequately prepared. If there were any sorry speeches made in this world they were made in the public speaking classes at Tech.

Finally Mitchell, in disgust, dressed down the whole class and said if there was not some originality shown he was going to fail everybody. He went on to say he was tired of listening to warmed over editorials from the local newspapers, and speeches based on some paragraph in one of the textbooks etc., etc., etc.

Well, the next class rolled around as usual. The roll was called and two men were absent, Bob Warner and Jack Phillips. Just as the first speaker was to take the stand the back door of the chapel opened and Bob Warner walked in. (The old chapel was where the Registrar's office is now and held about five hundred men.) Warner was dressed like the famous African explorer, Frank Buck, in khaki shorts, stockings, khaki shirt, pith helmet and boots. On his shoulder was a hunting rifle. He walked slowly down the aisle with everyone's eyes on him. He continued his stroll, walked up on the stage, sat his gun down, and began to talk. He started out by saying that he had just returned from Africa where he had been on a long safari that took him from the Cape of Good Hope to Cairo, thousands of miles on foot. He had been sent out by a group of scientists in Hamburg, Germany, he said, to find the link between the man and the monkey, known in those days as the Missing Link. Experts for years had been searching for the Missing Link and they felt that the time had come to settle this to the satisfaction of all. After describing the many vicissitudes of the trip, such as fighting great snakes, lions, wild elephants, insects, and inconveniences of life, he had, in the dense jungles of the continent, found and captured the Missing Link. Science had been proved correct and the Link actually existed.

The Link was twin monkeys or rather gorillas, which were white instead of the dark color you would expect. When the animals were captured they were talking to each other, and after a great struggle they were brought to heel and placed in cages to be returned to Hamburg where they attracted worldwide attention. He went on to say that Americans felt that they had to have their finger in the pie, so one Texas millionaire had purchased one of the Links for a tremendous sum of money and had brought him to this country where his habits, etc. were being studied. The only trouble was that the gorilla in Hamburg was pining away with a broken heart and the explorer decided he would search through America to find his simian brother. The gorilla in America had been hidden away in a secret lab, however, and no one was able to locate him or find anyone who knew anything about the situation. After an appealing speech Warner went on to say that to aid him in his search he had brought the gorilla with him from Hamburg. With that he walked to the back of the stage, threw back the old movie screen that had been hanging there for years, and there stood the monkey from Hamburg. He was nude except for a towel around his loins and was covered with hair. Being frightened by the light, he had a blank stare in his eyes. After a while, scratching himself as a monkey does, his eyes opened wide and a smile appeared on his face. He jumped from the stage, rushed up to Professor Cox, threw his arms around him and hollered "Brother!" Pandemonium broke loose and the monkey was given a big cheer. Finally, the class broke up leaving only Warner and Professor Cox, in Phillip's arms. Mitch gave them a lecture (a friendly

(Continued on page 83)

J. W. Heisman, Tech's first full-time professional coach who fired some of the schools greatest teams from 1904-1919.

W. A. (Bill) Alexander, head football coach at Tech from 1920-1944.

Robert L. (Bobby) Dodd, head football coach at Tech from 1944-1966.

Dr. Gilbert H. Boggs, professor of chemistry, from whose clutches Griffin barely escaped.

W. H. (Big Doc) Emerson, Georgia Tech's first dean.

Dr. D. M. Smith, head of the math department and a great friend of athletes. "If there was ever a pair of characters on this campus, D. M. Smith and W. A. Alexander certainly filled the bill."

Tech's greatest professor—Dr. John Saylor Coon.

Roy Mundorff of "Muddledorff"—"math professor, basketball coach, baseball coach, naval officer, big operator, you name it."

one) and said he appreciated the originality, but the next time anything like this happened in his class he was going to have the Dean send them both back home. Good luck.

A Letter of Interest

October 2, 1962

Dean George C. Griffin
Georgia Institute of Technology
Campus

Dear Sir:

I want to protest with all my might, strength, vigor, vim, and vitality, your awarding one Mr. Bob Eskew a trophy with the inscription, "The Greatest Tennis Player In The World."

First, I feel that my championship, duly won on the field of battle—and with all honor, has been sabotaged. I took a has-been, a player who has been out of college for several years, one Jack Rodgers, and through my ability and his perseverance, won a Championship.

The only other experience I've had with Mr. Eskew was on one occasion I took Claude Petty, who didn't know how to count the score—Mr. Eskew took "Jarring" *Jim* Wohlford, who has had professional training—Petty & Coleman defeated Eskew & Wohlford decisively. I leave it to your judgment as to who is the greatest.

I can only believe a typographical error was made, and it was intended, "The Poorest Tennis Player In The World."

In all indignation,
TONTO COLEMAN,
GA. TECH DOUBLES CHAMPION.

The Man From Detroit
Professor Dennison

As all of you know, Professor H. E. Dennison, director of the Industrial Management School, acted as coach of the golf team. This was one of Alex's ideas. He used several of the professors as part-time coaches, maybe to have a friend at court in time of trouble. Professor Bortell of physics coached the tennis team for many years, and George Griffin has been coaching the cross country team for over 40 years, etc. The moral of this story is to show how you can build yourself up to believe anything.

One day Professor Dennison invited one of the prominent businessmen of Detroit to come down and address his seniors just before graduation. The gentleman delivered a fine speech, and after lunch Professor Dennison invited him out to East Lake for a round of golf. They arrived at the club, caddies were hired, and they started out. The visitor turned to his caddy (since he did not want to call him boy or caddy) and asked his name. The lad said "Henry Four." The gentleman, not understanding, asked again. The lad again said "Henry Four." Again, the gentleman asked. Professor Dennison, overhearing the conversation, broke in and said "what he is trying to tell you is that his name is Henry Ford." "Oh," said the gentleman, "I've heard that name before." With that the caddy said "Boss, I spec you has, I have been caddying out here 17 years."

The Proposed Retirement of Dr. Crenshaw

One day Dr. Brittain, then our president, asked Dr. Crenshaw to drop by and see him. Old Herr Doc on his next trip to the main building or rather the Administration Building as it is known now, dropped in to see the president.

You fellows know Dr. Brittain. Before coming to Tech he was mixed up in old Georgia politics and when he talked to you he always finessed around without saying directly what he was trying to put over. It finally dawned on Dr. Crenshaw that Dr. Brittain thought it would be a good idea if Dr. Crenshaw retired at the end of the year. When the thought struck him, he jumped up out of his seat, grabbed Dr. Brittain by the lapels of his coat, and shaking his finger in his face said "look here old man, if you are talking about me retiring, come out in the hall and I will beat the hell out of you." (Doc was about eighty then.) You may rest assured that Herr Doc did not retire until he was good and ready.

A Little Girl on Skates

Before Coach Pittard came to Tech, he spent many years at Gainesville High School in Gainesville, Georgia acting as football and baseball coach. He turned out many fine championship teams.

Joe being a kind person, always ready to turn his hand for a friend, had, at the request of a few of the mothers, been bringing some of the teen-age daughters of his friends to Atlanta once every two or three months to shop at Rich's and Davison's.

Joe at that time owned an old Pontiac car which he had driven for years. He jogged along on the highway at thirty miles an hour, getting there, but at times the young people felt he would never make it. Finally one of the young ladies screamed, saying "stop, stop Mr. Pittard!" Joe pulled off on the shoulder, turned around and asked what was the matter. The little lady, daughter of the President of Brenau College said "Mr. Pittard, there is a little girl on skates who wants to get by." All Joe could say was "pshaw."

How Not to Judge a Good Baseball Player

When Lewis Hooks was in school (former captain of football and baseball) he had a friend in the student body by the name of Lane. At that time Lane was studying Mechanical Engineering each winter quarter and playing second base for the Cincinnati Reds during baseball season.

One day Lewis took Lane down to the dressing room and found the dirtiest uniform he could. The uniform had no rubbers in the legs, a rip in the back, and was badly in need of a bath. He took several of his friends into confidence, and they had Lane report to Coach Joe Pittard to try out for the baseball team. It was the first day of practice. Joe (better known as Humphrey Pennyworth) was holding forth, giving out instructions and so on, when Lane walked up. Joe said "son, what can I do for you?" Lane said he wanted to try out for the team. Joe surveyed him and his doubts arose, but he said "what do you play?" Lane told him second base. So Joe, trying to get rid of him in a hurry, told him to get out there. Joe took his trusty Fungo, which he carried with him everywhere, and started in on Lane. He hit Lane about a dozen, and Lane either booted them or threw them over the first baseman's head. Finally Coach Pittard shook his head and asked him to come on up and hit a few. Lane strode to bat and either struck out or fouled off each pitch. A weak roller to the infield was finally too much. Joe stopped the practice and called Lane up. He said he was sorry but Lane would have to turn in his uniform. "I don't believe you can make it." With that, pandemonium broke loose. Hooks and his pals rolled on the ground laughing and cheering. Joe looked blank until Hooks told him he didn't believe he knew a good ball player when he saw one. The next time you see Joe ask him if he knows a good player when he sees one and watch the sickly grin spread over his face.

Buck Flowers in Math Class

Old D.M. as we remember, Dr. D. M. Smith, really had a soft spot in his heart for athletes. He was terribly crippled, but according to some stories he had been a great athlete in college; maybe that was his interest. I know that the stories about his mathematical ability are true. He was one of the finest students Vanderbilt ever had and was a world-renowned mathematician.

He had a habit of asking all athletes to take their books and go to the board and work problem number nine. Then any athlete who worked problem number nine correctly caused every athlete to get a 100 for the day. This particular time, when the weekly announcement came about there were five athletes in the class and not a one moved. Finally Buck Flowers stood up, turned around to the others, pulled down his vest—yes, everyone wore coats, ties, etc. to class in those days—and said "come on fellows, I can make my 20." It did no good, so all received a zero.

Dr. Alexander

It is firmly believed among Alex's friends that he was a frustrated doctor. He always had a cure for anything. I'll never forget one day sitting in his office when Ralph McGill walked in. At that time Ralph was a roly-poly. He admitted to Alex that he was getting too fat and that he just had to reduce. That was all Alex needed. He snapped his fingers and said "I know just the thing—I'll put you on my potato diet." McGill was sucker enough to listen to Alex, and in two weeks he was so big he was about to explode. I used to see Ralph while he was writing about the integration problem, and would tell him to stop all that foolishness and write something interesting—write about the potato diet. He would always say no one would be interested in that. This is leading up to Boozer Pitt's experience with Dr. Alexander.

When Boozer was head coach at Auburn he came up to see Alex one day. They met at the old Atlanta Athletic Club building on Auburn Avenue where they had lunch. After a while Alex asked Boozer if he felt all right. Boozer then told the Coach he had an upset stomach, and Alex, pulling his usual line, snapped his fingers and said "I know just the thing." He called the waiter and asked him to bring a bottle of tabasco and a big tablespoon. The waiter soon appeared with the tabasco and the spoon. Alex opened the bottle, filled the tablespoon with tabasco, handed it to Boozer, and said "sip this." Before Boozer realized it he had swallowed the whole dose. It looked like lightning struck him. He jumped up as if he had been shot, grabbed a glass of water and started running around the dining room, hollering "water, water!" They handed him glass after glass, then a pitcher full. He downed everything handed him. Finally the pain subsided, and he sat down after wrecking the place. Alex asked Boozer "how do you feel now?" Boozer, afraid to say anything else because he didn't know what else Alex had up his sleeve, said "I am feeling fine." Alex said "I knew I could cure you."

Are the Boys Treated Fairly at Georgia Tech?

When the time came to integrate Georgia Tech everyone on the campus (that is among the faculty) began to talk to their students about their conduct when the first colored student registered at Tech. One day Professor Glenn Rainey was making a most serious talk to his class when one of the boys on the front row asked him if he thought professors would treat the Negro boys fairly when they became students at Tech. With that, one of the smart boys in the back spoke up and said "no, they don't even treat the white boys fairly."

The Mighty Dutchman

While shooting the breeze with Professor Fred Wenn the other day the subject turned to many characters that had attended this gristmill and, along with Spec Landrum, who was a most interested spectator, the subject of Old Dutch Konnemann came up. We finally decided that the only way Dutch ever stayed around the place for four years was because of his great sense of humor, which made people want to have him around. Dutch never graduated. In fact, even if he had wanted to he would not have had a chance. All this was brought about through something that happened during his sophomore year. Oscar Oldknow, who at that time was president of the National Theater Supply Co. with headquarters in Los Angeles, came over to Atlanta for Homecoming or some such celebration. He watched Dutch play, and after the game told Alex to tell Dutch that when he finished school he was to come to work for him. (Oscar had also been president of the Fox Film Corp.)

Alex kept the offer under his hat as requested by Oscar, and it was only about two weeks before the close of school during Dutch's senior year when Alex told Dutch that he was to go to work with Mr. Oldknow. Dutch was tickled to death. We didn't see Dutch for about two weeks. Finally one day I found him and asked why he was not in class taking his exams. His answer was that he didn't see any use in doing so since he already had his job and had been having a good time. One thing led to another. I saw Oscar two or three years later and asked him about Dutch. Oscar said they had 15,000 employees and Dutch was the dumbest one in the whole system, but they had to raise that rascal's salary three times since he had been with them. Dutch was finally sent to their Houston office. He did well but had his mix-ups as usual.

One night they left Dutch there in a big six-story building filled with millions of dollars worth of equipment. Dutch finally finished up about eleven p.m. and as he walked out, he failed to turn out the lights or to lock the front door. Later in the evening one of the Dallas police officers came along checking the front doors of the business houses and, lo and behold, the National Theater Office was wide open, the lights were on, and not a soul was in sight. He finally reached someone who came down, locked up the place and returned home. The next morning the boss sent for Dutch and dressed him down. Dutch took it like a man; when the boss finished, Dutch patted him on the back, told him not to mind for everyone made a mistake once, and politely walked out. What could the boss say?

When Dutch was in school, Alex had a terrible time keeping him here. Things finally became so bad that he hired Harry Strauss as more or less a bodyguard for Dutch, to see that he went to class, ate regularly, and at least opened a book. The first night Dutch, who was studying or supposed to be studying, said he had to go down the hall a minute. Out he went followed by Harry. He went inside the room, and Harry waited and waited, but no Dutch. Finally he decided to see just what had happened. He knocked on the door, walked in, and there was no Dutch. The room was on the first floor and Dutch had walked in, jumped out the window, and headed for town. From then on everywhere Dutch went, there was Harry.

One day there was a very prominent visitor on the campus. I

took him over to Brittain Dining Hall for lunch and as we were coming out, Dutch walked out behind us. I turned around and introduced him to the gentleman. With that, Dutch turned around and said to meet his shadow. Harry stepped from behind one of the pillars in front of the dining hall, met the gentleman, and then retired to the shadows.

One day while on a football trip to play the University of California, Alex took the team to Hollywood as guest of Mr. Frank Freeman who, at that time, was Executive Vice-President of Paramount Pictures Corp. While they were there, Bo Johnston came by the hotel to see the fellows and the coaches. About that same time Herman Adams also came by. Herman asked Bo what he was doing, and Bo said he was working for Warner Brothers. Herman asked how long he had been there, and Bo said it had been about a week. Herman then asked (Herman had hopes of following an acting career) how he had done it—he had been there three months trying to get in the front door and no one would even speak to him. So Bo told him this story. He had called up Warner Brothers and talked to someone in the personnel department, who first told him there was nothing doing. Finally it came out that Bo had been a basketball star at Tech. The man then asked who he knew in Los Angeles. Bo replied that he knew a fellow by the name of Dutch Konnemann. The man told him to come on out and he would give him a job. This was too much for Herman. It turned out that Dutch, while in Houston, had entertained this gentleman who was attending a theater meeting there. You never know, do you?

Tech Auto Department

(author unknown)

This story is especially for those men who took Machine Shop, and spent their time on this job.

The Automobile Department is nothing new at Tech, although there may be many who are not aware of that fact. It is not listed in the catalogue, owing to the fact that at present there is not enough equipment for a large number. The department has been in operation for several years, under the able direction of Gus Martindale, the Auto Expert, M.E. in A.E., from I.C.S. The course is a very thorough one, and not a single graduate has been known to be unsuccessful in landing a very lucrative position.

The machine now under construction has been given the name of Martindale "50." Where the "50" came from is a matter of dispute; supporters of the white and gold declaring that it refers to the number of years needed for completion, while the builder states that the machine is going to run about 50 miles (and then fall to pieces). At any rate, it is the original design of E. Benbow, and "belief me kiddo" (apologies to Frank Roman), it is going to be a bear kitty. As has been often stated, no effort is being made to make the machine a beauty; speed being the only end in view.

It will be remembered that two years ago the Drawing Department, represented by Pud, the Speed King, copped the bacon from the Shops Department, represented by Uncle Heinie, the Cyclonic Cyclist. Previous to this the Shops had never known defeat, and since, have bent all their efforts towards the recovery of the aforesaid bacon.

Under the leadership of Gus, the Auto Expert, the entire shop force, from Aunt Polly down to Woodshop Sam, have been putting their time and thoughts (no currency) on the construction of the Martindale "50." Meanwhile, Pud the Speed King, reigns supreme on North Avenue.

Among the more wealthy members of the faculty who have contributed to the Auto Department, we find Tobe, the Physical Phenomenon; Tommy, the Renowned Registrar; Quack, the Pill-slinger; and Gus Allen, the Hashmaker. The first three are the proud owners of Fords, and insist that there are none better. The last named should worry for expenses. He buys one at the beginning of one month, wears the very axles off of it, and by the beginning of the next month, he's got a new one. Ish Ka Bibble!

One day the Physical Phenomenon's car just absolutely refused to go. Investigation revealed the fact that there were dust particles on the crank handle. Quack gives his motor a No. 6 every morning, and has never been known to have had trouble. Tommy's registered Motor Vehicle has a perfectly regular schedule, and is always on the job. The Hashmaker's limousine is running nearly all the time. He takes a bunch of fellows to ride after each meal, feeling that as the fellows pay for his gasoline they are at least due a ride, even if they don't get anything to eat.

Secretary Adams, the Whirlwind Motorcyclist, who, by the way also gets his gasoline from the fellows, is the originator and founder of the Motorcycle Department. He intends to begin his fame by defeating the Cyclonic Cyclist, and then as a climax ease one over on the Speed King. Of course this last at present seems impossible, but the Whirlwind Motorcyclist has lots of confidence in himself, and states that he will be ready for the speed contention in the course of a few years.

It might be said here, that Tech is not going to stop at this point. "Pap" Adams of the Mechanical Section has expressed his intention of organizing the Aero Club. The first ship will soon be under construction, and strange to say, the Cyclonic Cyclist is going to furnish the material. Look out Speed King, the Cyclonic Cyclist is coming back.

(the machine was completed but never turned a wheel)

When Tech Annihilated Centre

It was a beautiful day toward the last of October 1920 that the far-famed team of Kentucky Colonels from Centre College came to Grant Field to do battle with the Golden Tornado. From one end of the country to the other it had been acclaimed as one of the great battles of the year and Centre was ruling a seven-point favorite.

Nineteen thousand fans gathered to witness the fray and nineteen thousand went wild when Buck Flowers put his toe to the ball and booted it 30 yards for a field goal after four minutes of play. It was a beautiful kick and the psychological effect of it proved invaluable to Tech's eleven.

At 3 to 0 the score stood at the end of the first quarter, the Colonels having lost their one and only good chance to score when they fumbled on Tech's 12 yard line toward the last of the first round. Then, after an exchange of punts in the second frame, Red Barron, playing with his jaws wired together, shot through right tackle for 55 yards and the first touchdown of the day.

The third quarter saw Tech still on the offensive with Centre plainly showing the telling effect of the Tornado's driving blows. Once in possession of the oval Centre resorted to the aerial attack, McMillen to Snoddy. Frank Ferst stepped in the way of one and broke it up and when 'Bo' tried it a moment later, the Tech quarterback snagged it. He started toward the goal, completing a 55 yard jaunt a few seconds later. Judy Harlan added the last tally of the day when he bucked the ball over in the fourth quarter. Big Bill Fincher came through with three extra points and the game ended 24 to 0.

Thus was defeated the mighty Centre team. For the first time in five years they were held scoreless, and for the first time in his life the mighty All-American McMillen was unable to move out of his tracks, much less to do any scoring.

This was probably one of the great historic games of Tech's football history. There have probably been one or two more games that approached this game, but as far as Atlanta was concerned, it just about disrupted the city. In many of the stores on Peachtree there was no one to wait on customers, everyone was out on the street talking about Bo McMillen, Tiny Roberts, Weaver, etc. These three men were unanimous All-Americans.

At that time Mr. George Adair was still alive. He would sit on the bench each Saturday, hardly moving a muscle, but he had to have his part in this game. He went to Coach Alexander and said, "Coach, I want to speak to the team before the game." The old man gave his permission and Mr. Adair's time came to speak. Here it is in a few words. "Boys," he said, "They call these people the Praying Colonels, but I must tell you that every man, woman, and child in Georgia is praying for you" and sat down. The only other time Mr. Adair ever became excited was at the Clemson game the week before. Alex started his second team, saving his varsity for the Centre game. The first quarter passed, no score (Tech was supposed to win by 29 points). The second quarter passed, no score. Then the third quarter came up, no score, here was a great season about to go by the board, the fans were excited and yelled and hollered for the first team. Finally Mr. Adair could not stand it any longer. He quit twisting his ring, got up, went up to Alex and said "Coach, how long have I known you?" Alex said, "For about 15 or more years." Mr. George said, "I have never asked you a favor in my life, have I?" Alex said, "no sir." Well, Mr. George said, "I am asking you one now, put the first team in." Alex said "Mr George, you go sit down, it is not right to do so right now." Mr. George returned meekly to his seat and said nothing. The fourth quarter rolled around, still no score. Finally just as the quarter ended Tech worked the ball down close to the goal. The signal was called, Pinky Hunt took the ball to run around right end, missed the signal, ran around the left end and scored. Tech had won 7 to 0.

The First Radio Dance

Sometime between the fall of 1919 and the spring of 1920, the first Radio Dance in the world was held at the Capital City Club on Peachtree Street in Atlanta. Arthur Murray, the great dance impresario, was a student at Tech at the time. The dance was a joint project of the Tech Band, the Georgia Tech Signal Corps ROTC unit and Arthur Murray. Leon Levy and Abel Winburn were Murray's orchestra. Both were members of the Georgia Tech Glee Club. Leon, who tells the true story in the following letter to Walter Coxe (an old classmate of ours who thought there was a good story in the first radio dance), later became one of America's greatest architects. He now lives in Sanibel Island, Florida, since retirement.

Dear Walter:
    I tender herewith my recollections of the Arthur Murray Capital City Club radio broadcast, as per George Griffin's request, in his

last report to the Class of 1922, which looked like it had been typed on a piece of stale bread.

However, the part about the broadcast was reasonably decipherable and, on account of it, I am emboldened to try my own luck on the typewriter, as I realize the anxiety with which the world is waiting for these advices.

Arthur Murray had a dancing class which he called "The Club de Vingt" (probably because it had sixty-five members) which met in the ballroom of the Capital City Club once a week.

He hired Abel Winburn and me as the orchestra; Abel to play piano and me to play the drums. We weren't very good but we were also very cheap, and the young folks in those days apparently lacked the critical faculties they have since developed about music.

They didn't dance too good either, which made it a Mexican standoff.

I recall that Abel and I got a dollar and a quarter a session, which lasted about three hours. This was good money. It wasn't much, but it was good. Besides, we were out of the high-rent district, since the club furnished the piano for Abel and I borrowed the drum from the Tech Band room. Frank Roman was unalterably opposed to anyone taking instruments off the premises, but he never objected to this, possibly because he didn't know about it.

Abel and I were happy to have the job, because if we hadn't been down at the Club de Vingt playing music, we would have been studying or going to classes, both of which activities were held in limited repute in the circle in which we moved.

On this historic occasion of which I write, the Tech Band (minus one drum) did broadcast, and the music was picked up at the club. There was only one set of ear-phones, trailing a long wire, and everyone took turns dancing with the phones clamped on, with the wire tripping up the rest of the dancers. They were thus able to hear the Tech Band play hundreds of choruses of "Ramblin Wreck."

They may also have played "Up with the White and Gold," but not while I was listening.

I remember remarking to myself that, while this new invention made the band sound worse than usual, it at least spared one the necessity of sitting there and looking at it. 1922 was a particularly good year for unlovely bandsmen. On this basis alone I predicted that radio would be a ringing success, and it was.

Of course, modesty forbids me to suggest that the Band's readings suffered by my absence from the percussion section, but the thought does occur to one, doesn't it?

Curiously enough, no one seems to have had the presence of mind to say something like Thomas Edison's, "What hath God wrought?", or, if they did, they didn't say it to me.

Actually, the thing I remember best was the subsequent spirited argument which ensued between Winburn and me on the one side, and Murray on the other. It was based on the latter's contention that the broadcast had taken up so much time that we hadn't played a dollar and a quarter's worth.

I forget who won, but in light of Arthur's accomplishments to date, I would be inclined to offer attractive odds that it wasn't the orchestra.

I have run into Murray on numerous occasions in New York, and he doesn't look any older than we were at Tech. Come to think of it though, he looked pretty old at that time.

So much for history.

The Battle of the Century

A good many years ago, the YMCA was having its troubles due mainly to the fact that there were quite a number of World War I veterans in school who were prejudiced against the Y at the time because of treatment received during the war. Things had gone from bad to worse and no one was attending the meetings. Several of the lads around the campus were asked to take charge of the situation and see what could be done to arouse a a little more interest in the work of the Y.

There were a couple of lads in school, one of whom was Bill Moses, a friend of the writer's, who were carrying on quite a feud. Nothing could be done to settle the situation, so they were approached with the idea of fighting it out before the student body. They both agreed and arrangements were made to have the fight in the old chapel (where the Registrar's office is now). The stage was fixed up as a boxing ring, a referee was appointed and seconds were secured. The bout was well advertised and we were ready. The night of the big battle approached. The Chapel was crowded and they were hanging from the rafters. The doors were locked and Moses and his opponent went at it. How the fight came out I have forgotten, though it seems it was a draw, and everyone shook hands. Friendship was re-established and everyone gave a big rah. Little did the spectators realize they were about to attend the largest YMCA meeting ever held at

Georgia Tech. Before the fight started the back doors were locked, so everyone was trapped. With much ado, the writer was called on to announce that we would now have a YMCA meeting and that Dr. Hull, a well known Bible student and lecturer, would speak to us. There was a little growling, but in those days boys were more polite (no dissenters) so they stolidly sat there and took their medicine. The meeting went off without too much trouble, but on the next day old Griffin really had to take it. The first greeting was how was my cousin, speaking of the then YMCA secretary. From there on out, the raspberries flowed fast and furious. Finally, like everything else, everyone began to see the humor in the thing and we are happy to say that the YMCA again became popular on the campus. But ever after that, no one was interested in a boxing match. It was the last one ever held on the campus at Georgia Tech.

Alex's Favorite Story

Many years ago, when prize fighting was in its heyday, many famous fighters were in the ring attracting attention from all over the world and winning championships galore. Some of these famous ones were Jim Corbett, John L. Sullivan, Bob Fitzsimmons, Jim Jefferies, and one of the most famous, Jack Sharkey.

As you remember, the fighters in those days fought for peanuts, and when it came time to train, they did the best they could. This was the case of Sharkey, who had a big championship fight coming up. He had no money to set up a training camp, so he took up over on Long Island and went to work. Every day after a ten or twelve mile run he would stop in a certain saloon right near the end of his run, buy a five cent glass of beer, then eat his lunch. Free lunch was the big selling point in those days and Sharkey would clean the counter.

Finally, one day the owner spoke to a friend of his and told him that Sharkey was about to break him. He would come each day after a long run, by a nickel glass of beer and eat everything in sight. He asked his friend if he had any ideas as to what he could do. His friend thought for a while and said that the next day instead of the free lunch, he should put a bowl of hardtack on the lunch table. This ought to cure him. So be it as it may, Sharkey finished his run, came in for his glass of beer and his lunch and, lo and behold, there was the hardtack. He immediately went to work, cleaned up the bowl, and then turned to the proprietor and said "now that we have had the tasties, where is the lunch?"

The Chimney Sweep

One of the greatest of our alumni is none other than Hazard Reeves, class of 1928 and Chairman of the Board of Reeves Broadcasting Co. and Reeves Industries of New York. Hazard is one of the pioneers in the sound industry and has won Oscars and other prizes for this work in the sound field. Like all fellows of his type, Hazard was fooling around with radio back in his student days; running wires, building sets and working on sound. One day he was on top of his fraternity house putting up an antenna, when all of a sudden he fell down the chimney. Unfortunately, some boys were sitting in front of the fireplace waiting to go pick up their dates. They were all spick and span in their tuxedos when a great burst of soot blew out of the chimney, covering them from head to foot. This was soon followed by none other than one Buzz Reeves. Well, the antenna was delayed somewhat in its construction because Buzz wasn't able to sit down for a few days after Nig Carson and Fish Davis got through with him.

Nig and Fish were a real couple of characters. I will never forget one day their dads came by their room at the fraternity house in which they were living. The room had not been cleaned up for weeks and newspapers were knee deep. Dirty clothes were all over the place. The beds were unmade and everything else was wrong. The dads went up to the room, knocked on the door and no one answered. They decided to go in. It took a lot of pushing to make it into this den of iniquity, but it wasn't long before it looked like a working party of a dozen men broke loose in that part of the house. Never again did Fish and Nig get caught.

Don't Be a Damn Fool

All the old timers remember Kid Clay, who for many years was a member of the coaching staff. He was freshman football coach, scrub coach, and head coach in baseball. It was under Kid that Tech had some of her finest ball teams and set records that have not been equaled since. As we all know, Kid was a feisty sort of little fellow. He put on a big act of being hard-boiled, but would give you the shirt off of his back. He was, I believe, trying to follow in Alex's footsteps.

One year he had the two worst managers in the world for his baseball team, LeBey and McDonough. They just about drove Kid crazy, along with Eddie Morgan who was the captain that year. For instance, the team would run out on the field at the beginning of an inning and LeBey and McDonough would refuse to throw them a ball. Eddie Morgan would get so steamed up that he would just about explode. One day after practice, LeBey and McDonough walked into the dressing room under the old East Stand and each had a handbag full of baseballs. Kid stopped them and said they were the sorriest managers he had ever had in his life. If he were them, he would quit right now. With that, McDonough and LeBey opened up their handbags, dumped the balls all over the dressing room and said they quit. Kid told them not to be damn fools. The next day they were back at their old tricks again, and managed to survive the season without losing their lives.

The Navy Never Gets the Word

One of the old Navy stories always bears repeating, so we will give it a whirl. As we all know, there is always a happy rivalry between the services, but we must admit that at times it gets a little beyond the fun stage.

It seems that when the Bonhomme Richard was having her famous fight with the British ship, the Serapis, many wonderful things happened. One was the Navy Motto which goes, "I have not yet begun to fight." As the battle raged, things became hotter and hotter. In those days three Marines took their stations in the top of the mast where they could shoot down on the deck of the enemy and kill those exposed. The ships were lashed together and the battle had been raging for several hours without result, when a cannonball from the Serapis cut the halyards flying the colors of the Bonhomme Richard. As the colors floated slowly down, they were noticed by the British Captain who took his speaking trumpet and asked Captain John Paul Jones if he surrendered. With that, John Paul Jones made his immortal reply, "I have not yet begun to fight."

The Marines, who had been hanging on the tops firing the red hot muskets and wondering when it would ever end, heard the reply. With that they threw their muskets down on the deck and said that was just like the damn Navy, they never get the word.

The Army Has First Choice

In reply to the John Paul Jones story, the Navy always came back with this one. You must remember this is an old hoary tale so please forgive us. It seems that a civilian ran into an old Army Colonel one day. They began to talk back and forth when finally the civilian asked the Colonel why was it that when you saw a lot of soldiers, you always saw a lot of mules, and when you saw a crowd of sailors, you always saw a crowd of Marines. The Colonel said that was easy. The Army had first choice.

To Bed to Bed Cried Sleepy Head

Old John Brewer finally fell in love. One day his girl came up to the campus to see him. He proudly showed her around the old school and, while telling her the usual stories about the old place, arrived at the corner of North Avenue and Cherry Street. In those days if you remember, there were two or three cottages where the Aeronautic building stands. There were only two real dorms, Knowles and Swann, on the campus at the time plus the two shacks. The school had grown so fast that sleeping space was at a premium on the campus, and one of the cottages at the corner of North Avenue and Cherry was rented as a temporary dorm. Well old Brewer had the room on the corner right at Cherry and North Avenue and as they passed the house, John showed her where his room was and asked her to come up on the porch so he could show her how he went to bed every night. She willingly went up on the porch and as she did, John lit out on the dead run and dove through the window. There was a terrible clatter, a big yell, a cry for help, and the running of other feet to the rescue. After picking John up and brushing him off, they returned him greatly embarrassed to his girl and everyone broke into a big laugh. One of his pals had heard him talking to his girl, slipped in the back way, run to John's room and moved the bed out into the middle of the room which, to everyone in the place, was a big joke but only a bug to our great baseball hero.

How Not to Stand an Inspection
But How to Make a 4.0 Without Half Trying

Right after World War I, when there was a little more patriotism left in the land, many of the fellows returning from the service signed up for ROTC. (Maybe it was because of the subsistence allowance. Money was mighty scarce in those days.) Anyhow, two of our great heros signed up again and started on a career as full-fledged members of the ROTC program. One had been a first lieutenant in the Rainbow Division, decorated for bravery, the other a top sergeant in an ammunition train, namely, Dummy LeBey and Bill Barnett.

Time for the annual inspection rolled around and you fellows who have been in the service remember the hurry and bustle necessary to get ready to knock the eyes out of the inspection party. Such was the case in the artillery unit under Major Washington.

The day of the inspection came and the inspection party started visiting the various classes, finally making its way to Major Washington's class. Attention was called, and everyone snapped to attention except our two heros who were sitting on the back row, feet on the seats ahead, asleep. (I hope they were.) Major Washington was terribly embarrassed and had them on their feet right away. After blustering around, the Colonel in charge started in on our two friends. The first question he asked LeBey was all about the handling of an artillery battery. Well, LeBey started in and bowled the old man over. The Colonel jumped on Barnett next and asked all about ammunition trains. Of course, the same thing happened. These guys knew more than the Colonel. Finally, the old man shook his head, turned to Major Washington, and said "Major, this is the best instructed class that I have ever inspected," and walked out with his party. After the inspection, Major Washington asked LeBey and Barnett to remain after class and he congratulated them on their performance and dismissed them.

For several years I tried my best to pin those rascals down, but, from Major Washington on down, they all insisted it was only an accident because no one knew what questions the Colonel was going to ask, so there was no chance of a frame-up. This is one story I have never believed.

The Absent-Minded Professor

No one knows why professors are so absent-minded. The only answer I can find is the fact that they are thinking up different ways to pass out those F's. I hope none of them read this.

Old Earl Bortell, who was for many years professor of Physics, friend of all the boys and nursemaid for the athletes in that easy course, ranked right at the top along with Dr. Crenshaw. One night Mr. and Mrs. Bortell were invited out for dinner and bridge. They had a very nice time, but it was necessary to leave young Earl at home with a maid who acted as baby-sitter, which worked to the satisfaction of all. Then came the rub.

After they had walked in from the party, Mrs. Bortell asked Earl to take the baby-sitter to the carline. They got into the car and drove the mile or so to the carline, but when they arrived the good professor did not stop. He just turned around and drove back to the house. They drove up into the driveway and stopped. Just as he was about to open the door of the car, the maid spoke up and said "Professor Bortell, what do I do now?" Old Earl was floored. He turned around and asked "what are you doing still here?" Poor maid, I hope she finally made the car.

Earl was also a great chicken financier. His success with the chickens was not as great as it was in dishing out the dope on MV square over 2. For several years Messrs. W. K. Hatcher and Jim McNeese allowed us to use their fishing camps, one at Lake Blackshear near Americus, and the other on the St. Johns river near Palatka. One weekend Jim McNeese invited us down to Lake Blackshear. Four or five of us arrived ready to catch all the fish in the lake. The first funny thing that happened was when, upon arrival, I went into the kitchen and opened the refrigerator. It was filled with big fish. I asked Clay, the caretaker, what did this mean. He said Mr. Jim and Mr. Henry (Henry Collier) had been down to Jim's place at St. Mary's and caught all the fish and left them for us. Clay said he knew the city slickers wouldn't catch any and he didn't want them to starve. How true.

We remained there two days. Friday it rained all day, Friday night the same, and it was still raining Saturday morning, but beginning to slack. Finally the sun came out about ten a.m. I said let's go. Bortell and Prosser, the world's greatest fisherman, said they were not going until they caught a fish. Finally, about 11:30 Bortell caught a small crappie about 8 or 10 inches long and so we decided to move out. While we were packing Bortell said he hoped it hadn't rained in Atlanta because his wife said if she had to go out in the rain and collect the eggs one more time he was out of the chicken and egg business. Well, when

Earl arrived home and walked into the house his eyes popped out. Every dish in the drawing room was filled with eggs, every dish and vase in the dining room was overflowing. The refrigerator was full. Pans were full. It looked like it had been raining eggs and that was the finish. The next day our physics professor was running around Buckhead trying to liquidate the Bortell chicken business, selling some of his two dollar and a half hens for sixty cents. How true the old saying "never underestimate the power of women."

Bortell, more or less as a hobby, coached the tennis team winning 100 matches over the years including the Southeastern Conference Championship on occasions. He had many great players during his career as coach, Billy Reese, Russell, Bobbitt, Frank Willett, Howard McCall, Ned Neely, and Harry Thompson being some of the outstanding Tech players. One of the better lads was Hank Crawford. Hank, while not number one by any means, was a terrible fighter and in a match was hard to lick. I remember one day Tech was playing Alabama. Alabama had not lost a match in four years and it was nip and tuck. Bill Reese had slaughtered their number one man and the rest had won two or three of the other matches and finally the match rested on just how Hank would come out. Old Bortell was about to have a fit, chewing on that cigar and about to walk himself to death. Finally he slipped up to Hank and asked "Hank, how are you doing?" Hank said he won the first set and it was 5-1 in the second in favor of Alabama, but for him not to worry. Well, doggone, if he didn't win the second set 7-5 and give his opponent a good cleaning in the third set.

Probably the most outstanding job a Tech tennis team did in all its years was in 1964. Earl took the team to Knoxville for the annual Southeastern Conference Championships. Tulane was the odds-on favorite, but when the finals rolled around Tech had a man in the finals in every classification. The only way for Tech to win was to win each class, one through five. Neely started the ball rolling by winning the number one group, and the individual championship, therefore, came to the Southeastern Conference. He and Thompson won the doubles also. This set the rest of Tech on fire. They really outdid themselves, winning every match and the team championship, one of Tech's greatest athletic victories.

Bortell was quite a player himself and won the Faculty Championship on several occasions. One year Coach Dodd beat him. That really checked him out, so the next year rolled around and they went after it hammer and tongs. The match lasted about three hours and attracted quite a crowd. Bortell finally won; in fact, we all accused Dodd of knocking the ball over the fence on occasions so he could get a little rest.

Golf is the Name of the Game

There is a certain fellow on the campus whose name will have to remain a mystery to all. Anyhow, one day during the summer Burdell II appeared on the campus, walking by the dressing room looking for Burdell I. These young bucks were both fine golfers, and with nothing much to occupy their time that summer they played a lot of golf, looked for fish under rocks, and all and all were having a great time. Burdell II asked Burdell I if he had any money. Burdell I said he had about $75.00 and Burdell II, having about the same amount, decided they would pool their resources and go to Highlands to find one of those millionaires and win some money. No sooner said than done. They packed, jumped in their car and headed for Highlands. After securing a room, they changed to their golfing costumes and appeared at the first tee. Well, by golly, there was no one around, and there they sat forlorn and wishing for a game. Finally, down the road came a squatty fellow about 55 years old, dressed in a white shirt and white ducks, the cuffs covered with red clay. He looked just like old Bortell who had a bad habit of walking on the cuffs of his tennis britches. They struck up a conversation with him, and after awhile they suggested playing a game of golf.

After much dickering the two Burdells decided they would give the old man two strokes a side. They started the game, and at the end the old man had beaten their best ball one-up and taken a third of their money. After a long palaver, they decided they would meet again that afternoon and they would only give him one stroke a side. When the game finished the old rascal had beaten them again, one-up. Well, by that time another third of their money was gone, so another match was arranged for the next morning, and there would be no strokes given. Again, the old hand won. This was the end. Here they were at the Highlands Country Club with a big bill staring them in the face, no gas and no money.

The funny part about the whole thing was that no one had mentioned their names to each other because they were so intent on the game, but lo and behold after the matches were over names were passed around and it turned out that the little, awkward old fellow was one of the outstanding golfers in Georgia who had not been playing much except when he was at his summer home in Highlands. Well, after a great debate it was decided that the only thing they could do was to call "The Boss" Burdell at the campus and have him stand for their bill with a little loan besides to get them back to Atlanta. I kid old Burdell I about this every once in awhile, and he does not deny the story but always says "Griffin, that tale is only half true."

This same Burdell I was more or less absent-minded at times, which caused him some rather embarrasing moments. One day there was a gentleman standing at the door of the dressing room and as everyone came by he stopped him and asked him if he was Mr. Burdell I. The question, after about 30 people had passed, finally found pay dirt. Burdell I came along and listened to the question and said yes, he was Burdell I. The man said "well, I have a warrant for your arrest." Burdell I turned white and ran over in his mind exactly what he might have done that would justify his arrest. The deputy said he had rented a battery several weeks ago and made no attempt to return it, and the company wanted the battery and the amount of the bill. Burdell swallowed and asked how much was the bill. The deputy said $86.00, and that brought on another chill. Well, anyhow, things worked to the satisfaction of all and all remained friends.

The next thing that happened was Burdell was found running

all over the campus all excited. He was finally stopped and asked what in the world was the matter. He said he couldn't find his car and that he had been looking for it for two days. Finally, one of his pals found it near the garbage dump by the dining hall where he had left it after not being able to find a parking place. I'll tell you he was something.

Don't Call Me Charlie

This day of such things as freedom of choice and freedom under the law reminds me of a story that John Staton told us one day at a meeting. It seems that just before the battle of El Alamein during World War II, the Commanding General of the Australian Forces received word that Lord Auchincloss, Commander in Chief, would be in Africa to inspect the Australian Army. As we all know, the Australians are worse than the Americans when it comes to freedom of choice, bowing to discipline, etc. The General decided he had better gather all of his forces together, which he did. He erected loud speakers all over the field they had selected, and the next day the entire Army paraded before him, lined up, and he mounted the platform. He told them that Lord Auchincloss, the Commander-in-Chief of his Majesty's forces, would inspect them the next day. He wanted them to polish their shoes, shine their buttons, and square their hats, and as long as Lord Auchincloss was there "don't call me Charlie."

You Have Never Seen Me Before

When Al Staton first went to work for the Coca-Cola Co. (soon after his graduation) he was sent to Providence, Rhode Island to represent the company. Part of his job was to sell Coca-Cola. All of the ball parks, race tracks, etc. were controlled by one of the old-time politicians. Al couldn't get to first base with him. He made call after call, but no soap. Finally, after one of his calls, the old man observed that Staton was a mighty big fellow and asked had he played football. This was a foolish question to ask one of the greatest players in the country, but Al just said yes. Well, the old man said, he owned a football team in Providence called the Providence Steam Rollers and they needed a tackle. He told him if he could go out and make the team, he could sell Coca-Cola anywhere in the state of Rhode Island. This was no job; Al went out and was soon the regular tackle on the team. The first game was against the Can Bulldogs, Jim Thorpe's team. The game started and Al was in his glory. The first play from scrimmage was an end run by Thorpe. Al broke through and threw Jim for a five-yard loss. Jim got up, patted Al on the back, and said "son, let old Jim run—that's what the folks came to see." The same play was tried again and the same thing happened, only this time Jim added "if you don't let old Jim run, I am going to knock you out." Jim was as good as his word. He came storming around end, hit old Al and knocked him crazy as a cuckoo. To add insult to injury the next game was against the Philadelphia Eagles, and the star tackle on the Eagles was none other than Sully Montgomery of the famous Centre College Praying Colonels. The kick-off passed and they lined up for the first play from scrimmage. Just as the ball was to be snapped, Montgomery raised up in the line, took time out, and spoke to Al saying "friend, haven't I seen you somewhere before?" Al looked around, couldn't find Dummy LeBey and Bill Fincher and as discretion was the first law said "no, it must have been someone else." (They had given Sully a good going-over in the Centre game.) Three times during the game Sully took time out, asked the same question, and received the same answer. Finally when the game was over he left shaking his head, wondering what had happened to his memory. Al dressed and beat it away as soon as possible, because the meeting would have been disastrous.

Life's Most Satisfying Moment

When World War II started, Al Staton was the Vice-President of Coca-Cola Export Corp. As were all men, Al was interested in offering his services to the country and was given a commission as Major in the U.S. Army. Later promoted to Lt. Colonel, Al was assigned to the 14th Air Force in Europe and devised the plans for the bombing of a great part of Germany. Since he had lived in Germany and at the start of the war was interested in a Coca-Cola plant in Hamburg, he was familiar with industry throughout that part of Europe. This is really incidental to the story.

When Al was at Tech, they revived basketball on the campus. They had a team at Tech around 1909, 1910 and for a few years thereafter but then interest waned and the sport died out. I remember looking up a few records of that era and found that Georgia beat Tech 79 to 8, and Al's team lost to the Macon Blues in Macon one night, 44 to 4.

Practice first started outdoors, then Alex finally had a little court built next to the YMCA building—three sides and no roof. The team struggled through for several years by practicing and playing their games at the Atlanta Athletic Club. To the dismay of all, Al Staton and Bill Fincher reported for the team. Both were great football players. Albert was All-Southern tackle for three years, and Bill All-American. Their basketball ability was at a low ebb but they were tremendous in size, and their lack of ability came in handy in those days when the game was so rough. One day right after World War I, the team was invited to play the Fort Benning officers at Columbus.

Tech reported for the game. The court was in an old barracks converted into a basketball court. The goals were at each end of the court over a couple of swinging doors on springs. When you pushed them to enter or leave and turned them loose, they swung back into place at once. Well, Al and Bill had a field day on the little court. They bounced the little lieutenants around off the little stands, slammed them to the floor and had a great time.

In those days the big shot in basketball was a set shot. Al was all set to make one when disaster took place. There was one little second louie who had taken a great deal of punishment, and he kept hoping something would happen where he could get even with the big cows. The opportunity had arrived. He saw Al all set to take that shot, when he noticed he was close to the door and it was raining cats and dogs outside. He couldn't let the opportunity slip. He came down the floor with full power and hit Al in the back. Al flew through the air, through the door, which swung open, and disappeared. About thirty seconds later the doors almost flew off their hinges and Al came storming in covered with mud. He spied his enemy and started chasing him around the court, but never caught him again. The game finally ended. Tech won and returned home.

Things rolled along for years and the game was forgotten, but things come back to curse you, so it overtook Staton again. When the big drive started in World War II and the heavy bombing raids took place which led to the end of the war, Al's outfit took one of the leading parts in the attack. Finally when the worst was over and Al was sitting in his office at the air field in England one day, the door opened and a two-star general stepped in. The general stated that it was customary when a man is decorated to have a formal ceremony, but due to the great confusion existing at the time it was felt best to handle the ceremony by having the general come down and decorate Al personally. The general took out the medal, and Al being somewhat confused and a little flustered, which was rather unusual for him, asked what it was for. The general immediately replied "Colonel, you remember many years ago at a basketball game played at Fort Benning in an old barracks right after World War I?" Al said "yes, sir." "Well, this medal is to reward you for one of life's most satisfying moments. I am the lieutenant who hit you in the back during the game and ran when you started chasing me." Then he pinned the medal on Colonel Staton. The general went on to read the citation praising Colonel Staton for the plans devised for the bombing of Germany, telling how successful they were and that his system had been adopted by the other air squadrons.

So all's well that ends well.

The Proof of the Pudding

This story from the 1912 *Blue Print* is about two of Tech's most famous faculty members. Both were characters.

No, gentle reader, this is not an advertisement for the Hupmobile, but a very good likeness of Pud, the Speed King. Besides correcting bulls in the drawing hall, he has other duties, one of which seems to be to tear up Atlanta's perfectly good streets and roads. In his younger days he could be seen every morning, with clock-like regularity, pedaling his way towards the Tech campus. One's breath was almost taken away watching him streak down North Avenue.

Nor was he the only member of the faculty who rode a bicycle, for, trailing by his side, there appeared another image—that of Uncle Heinie, the Cyclonic Cyclist. These friendly morning rides unfortunately developed into a bitter rivalry, surpassing even that exhibited by Tech and Georgia.

Everything went along smoothly until Uncle Heinie decided to enter the International Six-Day Bicycle Race. He immediately began training and no longer could they be seen side by side, but far in the rear, enveloped in a cloud of dust, could be seen the red face of Pud, the Speed King. Pedal as he might, the Speed King soon saw that he could not overcome the advantage possessed by Uncle Heinie. This advantage lay in the luxuriant beard of the Cyclonic Cyclist which, when thrown to the winds, produced an acceleration beyond the power of human ability to overcome.

As the rumbling thunder succeeds the lightning's flash, so did the furious imprecations hurled by Pud follow in the wake of Uncle Heinie. Do you think, even for a moment, the Speed King acknowledged defeat? NEVER! Right here the real "come-back" spirit showed itself. Plan after plan was considered and, finally, the automobile was decided upon as the machine, for it would take a machine to overcome the Cyclonic Cyclist, to bring him back his usurped rights. To be sure, an automobile would cost lots of money, but what is money against one's honor! The tailor's bill must be reduced, and reduced it was. Finally, after months of saving, the dream became a reality.

The whistle had blown ten minutes before, and still no clang of the bell in the wood-shop. Anxiety showed itself upon the faces of all the Subs, while Uncle Jake made use of a double chew of "Schnapps" to sustain his nerves. Where was Uncle Heinie? The excitement had almost reached its zenith when there was heard the thud, thud of weary footsteps mounting the stairs. In came a drooping figure, haggard and worn. It was Uncle Heinie. Upon seeing the ghastly face of the Cyclonic Cyclist, Uncle Jake dismissed the Subs and called the Shop's Force together. In came Mr. Billy, Horace Thompson, and the rest; while Woodshop Sam gazed sympathetically on from behind a post.

The head of Uncle Heinie was bowed in the realization of ignominious defeat. "Boys," said he, "I have met my Waterloo. I started out as usual this morning, and hit up a clip that I had never been able to do before. I had almost finished my course when my ears became filled with 'an hellish' noise. Nearer and nearer it came until, suddenly, it flashed by me—a veritable streak of smoke. Turning my head for an instant, I recognized the beaming face of my bitter rival, Pud, the Speed King. Upon my reaching the campus he confronted me with a paper on which was written the statement that he would torment me with his speed and so tear up North Avenue that it would be in no condition for me to ride my bicycle. Fellow-Shopmen, what are we to do?"

With an air of supreme confidence, Gus Martindale stepped forward and declared his intention of defending the honor of the Shops. He is now engaged upon the building of a machine which will be known not on account of its beauty but for its speed. He is spending day and night, but no money, upon this device. However, until it is completed, Pud, the Speed King, will reign supreme on North Avenue.

Tech's Greatest Professor

Tech's greatest professor, Dr. John Saylor Coon, was born in Burdett, New York in 1854. He graduated from Cornell in 1877, was a charter member of the ASME, held the Chair of Mechanical Engineering at Georgia Tech from 1891 until 1923, and died in 1938 in his home state. This information was picked up from Roddy Garrison's little book about Doctor Coon which he published in 1945 and mailed to each member of the ME class of 1923. He was, as Roddy said, mourned by those of us who knew, loved, and revered him. While I was not an ME, I used to go and visit his classes just to hear him lecture.

At times it was really amusing. Every year he had a stooge or straight man in his class. One year Jack McDonough was his straight man (Jack was later president of the Georgia Power Co., also chairman of the board). In the first place everyone wore a collar, tie and coat to class and, in the second place, when you recited you had to rise, not slouch in your seat. I can hear him now. He would say "Mr. Thomas (Dan Thomas), how do you open a steam valve and I don't want your ideas but a technical answer." Mr. Thomas would start out. About the middle of his recitation Dr. Coon would ask Mr. McDonough what Mr. Thomas was saying. Mr. McDonough would say "Doctor, he is saying nothing"; and Dr. Coon would say "you are wrong, Mr. Donough, he is saying less than nothing; sit down, Mr. Thomas."

Coach Alex use to tell me about Dr. Coon and the first automobile that came to Atlanta. It seems that for years when anything new in the engineering line was shipped into Atlanta, Dr. Coon was called upon to inspect the engine or article and give his approval. When the first automobile came to Atlanta, the owner called Dr. Coon and asked him to come out and go over the machine and see what the he thought of it. He went right out, came back to class and made the following announcement. "Young gentlemen, I have just seen a machine to which they have harnessed many horses. It smells like a Chinaman, runs like hell and they are going to give it to all the college students, women and colored delivery boys to drive. They are going to kill more people than all the wars in history." What a prophet.

Again, he was called on by the Georgia Power Co. to come down and inspect a new engine that they had just purchased. He dutifully went down, looked it over carefully and gave it his approval. But just as he was walking away, one of his former students decided to have a little fun with the good doctor and asked "Doctor, how long will this engine last?" He turned around in disgust, looked at one of his old boys, and said "twenty-one years, young man." Ben Sinclair, one of the Tech boys, later Chief of Construction for the Power Co., said the engine lasted 21 years and four months.

One day, to try and play a trick on Dr. Coon, the boys went by Uncle Heinie's and picked up a little furniture glue and glued a penny to the floor right in front of the long counter that Dr. Coon used as a desk. Dr. Coon saved almost anything that might prove of value, so when he finally spied the penny he walked around and tried to pick it up. Well, the fellows were about to bust as he fooled around trying to get it up but were afraid to laugh, not knowing what might happen. Without saying anything Dr. Coon straightened up and walked out of the room. After awhile he came back, got down on his knees, reached in the side pocket of his coat, and took out a hammer and a cold chisel. He chiseled the penny up, picked it up, put it in his pocket, turned around and took up his lecture where he had been when interrupted just as if nothing had happened. Well, the boys were really nonplussed and it was only after class that they busted out laughing but still wondered what had happened to their joke.

Each year Dr. Coon would go down to the Florida Keys for a vacation. There was a very fashionable place near Key West where many wealthy people visited for the fishing. Dr. Coon was a great fisherman and a man with a little side income from stocks. He would save his earnings from his stocks, and go down and spend a month trying to catch Sailfish and Marlin. One day he was out fishing. Being such an interesting man, he was a great favorite with all the men; therefore, they spent a great deal of time at his cottage. Since he was not there some of the gentlemen wanted a highball, so they had the bell boy from the main lodge bring down several. When Dr. Coon came back he walked up on the porch saw the drinking and asked WHAT WAS GOING ON THERE. Well, the party broke up right away. Everyone made their excuses and left. A little later the bell boy came down and said Dr. Coon, the manager would like to see you in his office. Dr. Coon reported as requested, and the manager said "Dr. Coon, I'm not allowed to tell you who said this, but I have orders to tell you that you can remain at this resort at no expense as long as you wish."

Dr. and Mrs. Coon had an old maid who had been with them for years and she was really just like a member of the family, but like all families she became angry at Dr. Coon about something one time and decided she was going to get even with him. (Remember this was back in 1919-29 when prohibition was in effect and they had the search and seizure laws which were so unpopular.) The maid goes down and reports Dr. Coon for having whiskey in his house, so the prohibition officers came out to search his house and found a quart of liquor. A great scandal. Dr. Coon was cited. His case came up in the federal courts, which attracted great attention in our city and the court room was filled with spectators; in fact, the SRO sign was out long before the trial started. Well, according to the way I picked the story up the baliff rapped for order and called Dr. Coon's case, but Dr. Coon was not there. There was a great calm when the Doctor did not appear. Finally, the swinging doors in the back of the courtroom almost came off their hinges and **Dr.** **Coon** came stalking down the aisle, talking in a loud voice, and saying "your honor, that's the bottle of whiskey Jack Spalding gave me twelve years ago and I want it back." Well, the great Federal Judge was flabbergasted. Never had he run into such an occasion, so he picked up the bottle—by that time the good Doctor had reached a position right under his rostrum—and said "Doctor, I'm sorry," and handed **Dr. Coon** the bottle of liquor. According to **Dr. Smith** there was a little byplay by one of the government attorneys trying to antagonize **Dr. Coon.** Finally, **Dr. Coon** spoke up and said "young man, I don't know who you are, but I know *what* you are." That was the end of the game.

For years **Dr. Coon** would not attend a football game. He thought it was played by a bunch of roughnecks; hence, he wanted nothing to do with a game that attracted that type of person. Finally, one day he was prevailed upon to go down and watch a game. The next morning while going to class he passed Jim Senter on the steps of the second floor of the ME Building. He stopped him and said "Mr. Senter, a man can still be a gentleman and play football." This brought about a great change in **Dr. Coon's** life. If some of you remember, the old West Stand had a little roof that extended over the last eight or ten rows of the stand. Well, **Dr. Coon** had a chair placed on top of the roof and until the day he left Tech he watched the game from up there and no one else was allowed up there but **Dr. Coon.**

Dr. Coon was a great fan. At all the home baseball games he sat in a private chair right next to the players bench. He would come to all track meets. In fact, I believe **Dr. Coon** was the only man Coach Alex was afraid of. When I first started coaching the track team, Alex was always on the field. One day the meet was supposed to start at two p.m., and at five minutes 'til two Alex told me to call the 100 yard dash, which was the first event in a dual meet. So at five minutes 'til two I started the 100 yard dash. At exactly two p.m. **Dr. Coon** walked into the stands and asked one of the lads where the 100 yard men were and why they were not lined up to run. The student told him they had already run the 100. So with that **Dr. Coon** walked onto the field, asked Alex to look at his watch, and gave him a good dressing down about not being on time. From then on I would say "Alex, its time to start" and he would always ask if Dr. Coon was in the stands. If I said yes, he would say go ahead.

One day I was riding down North Avenue with Alex. He had an old four-door Ford Model T Sedan, a showcase on wheels. Dr. Coon hated automobiles plus the fact that Alex was not much of a driver. As we passed by, Alex spied Dr. Coon on the corner of West Peachtree and decided to pick up the good doctor. Dr. Coon sat down in the back, and as we approached Spring Street there was a tapping on the window. Alex slowed down and Dr. Coon said "Alex, I'll just walk the rest of the way."

One day at commencement, one of the mothers of a graduate met Dr. Coon and said she was very happy to meet him and she understood that he was the head of the Mechanical Engineering School and her son's professor. Much to the lady's amazement, Dr. Coon said "no, madam, I am a professor of ethics at Georgia Tech." Dr. Coon always said and preached to his boys that the engineer should be the most honest man in the world. He is trusted with so much money and the safety of so many people depend on his designs, that cheating here and there risks the lives of too many people not to be honest and conscientious about one's work.

Here is what R. H. Lowndes (Class of 1903) had to say in the preface of Roddy Garrison's little book.

> No man was ever possessed of finer innate wisdom than was this man. His insight into the everlasting truths of nature, his interpretation of those truths, and his lifelong constancy in the proper adherence to them were outstanding characteristics in him, and showed themselves in his every action and utterance. His deep-seated love of nature, his fearlessness of the naked truth made of him a man who at once enjoyed living with other living creatures (the birds, the wild beasts, and, of course, the trees, shrubs, and his beloved rose bushes) and who at the same time delved into the scientific researches of the minds of men. He held no brief for "easy, popular thinking," for superstitions of the present brought down to us from unverified traditions of a groping past. He, as he himself expressed it, preferred to live under the laws of Almighty God, the unfaltering, unswerving, immutable laws of nature, rather than to live under the laws of man—the ever-changing, erroneous,

and incomplete laws of man which each succeeding legislature must of necessity alter.

Dr. Coon was first of all a man born with innate mental ability. This very ability enabled him early in life to see the necessity for mental training. He thus early became a student, nor did he stop his studies so long as his active life continued. Rather did he spend his life disseminating those studies. He spent many years in a deep and sincere effort to pass on to the future generations the blessed truths, which must and will rule the Universe, in the firm belief that by so doing he was rendering his fellow man the greatest benefit that lay within his power to render.

Dr. Coon had many flattering offers during his years of teaching, offers to take part in the industrial procedures of engineering; but he declined these offers because he preferred to remain among "his Boys," even at the meager salary of a school teacher, rather than give up his zeal to inculcate in the youth of the land the desire and necessity of thinking and the pleasure to be derived therefrom.

As he said to one of his classes, after he had just declined a lucrative offer, "Will I go? I will not! I prefer to live among young people, you boys, whose hair I ruffle, and whom I drag down and mop the floor with, and often seem to hammer a bit too hard (then maybe it is hard enough). But you must remember that the best steel which engineers make use of comes out from under the hammer."

It was the expert hand of genius which controlled this "hammer," and his students loved him the more for his use of it. Each blow left improvement in its product. The young men felt and knew this daily improvement. So much so that one of his most apt students told Dr. Coon, upon the completion of his studies at Tech, that his senior year, spent in daily contact with Dr. Coon, was the most inspiring, most edifying, and altogether the happiest year of his life, be it past or future.

Truly here was a man who spent his life in behalf of his fellow man.

A Few of Dr. Coon's Sayings

Reprinted by permission of R. R. Garrison, Class of 1923

Two of our boys have fallen out concerning Atlanta's new viaduct. One of them contends that the viaduct is hardly capable of sustaining the present loads it is subjected to—not to mention the future. It isn't written in the books you know, that trucks twenty years from now won't weigh more.

I'm an engineer on the Pennsylvania Railroad—I lower a boot down in a track tank while the train is traveling at 45 miles an hour. How should the mass of water be started? I want a technical answer to that question! If you don't know that instinctively, just write the folks back home and tell them as soon as the ground is right you are coming back and help them plant corn. I'll bet twenty-five dollars there is not a man in this big class who can tell me! "Mr. Borum, do you know?" Borum—"I think so, Doctor!" "Well, he may! Howcum nature to do that?"

Correct deportment is more essential than ability. Unless you are well-behaved because you want to be, you will slip up on the job. If a man breaks down his own ideals of honor, he is gone.

The greatest civilizer in the world, bar none, is properly conducted business.

One source of Wealth is raw materials, the other Labor.

The woes of the past have been caused by the determination of the strong to gather into their hands the profits of labor.

Heat is gold. What can be done to conserve your heat—heat from the earth—heat from the Sun? Have a sense of moral responsibility and leave to posterity, conditions.

Pursue such a course in life as will bring pleasant memories, for upon that depends a successful life, both spiritual and mental.

There is a great difference between ingenuity and brains. Genius is nothing but the will to take pains. Boys, patience is genius.

Engineering is common sense first, and mathematics, next.

Don't go blindly about the world, but try to find out the reason for things. Be observant.

Man is not a reasoning animal, with a passion for generosity and justice. He is simply a prejudice on two legs.

Men are moved by expediency. If I were tried for an offense, I would rather have boys of your age to sit as jurors.

Why is it advantageous to have a heating plant placed lower than position of heating system? —a technical answer will do. Mr. DuBose knows just as well as I do the answer to that question. Don't tell them, Mr. DuBose. Let 'em stew in their juice!

Knowledge comes from reflection. Learning comes from books.

What makes a bicycle stand up? (You just mull over that, I'm not going to tell you.)

Dr.: How do you determine the consumption of steam from an indicator card?

Student: You first multiply by the hyperbolic log and then . .

Dr.: Yes, and then kick it twice and divide by abracadabra.

Abracadabra—meaningless babble!

Mr. Carter, what are you doing? Eating candy?

All right, eat your candy, Mr. Carter.

Mr. Black, what causes the hammering in a steam pipe? I want a technical answer. Mr. Black thinks he knows, but he doesn't— that's right, laugh with them, Mr. Black you are too good-natured. You know no more about the subject under discussion than a wild jackass's colt.

Mr. Edwards, what is it that give a train $\frac{1}{2}mv^2$? If you say coal, I'll wring your neck and throw you out of that window! I want a technical answer.

With liberty goes immense obligations. Liberty imposes great obligations of fairness. Free speech should not extend beyond statement of fact. Statement of fact is either true or false. The world is full of opinions.

The conflict going on now between men who have knowledge and men who have opinions, is as old as time.

Boys, ignorance is very popular!

Man has been most insistent about things he could not prove.

What happens to the engineer if he makes a mistake in his delving—in the realm of spirit and truth? What happens to a surgeon? An artist? He can conceal his mistake!

When an engineering structure fails, a man's head should be cut off.

About a thousand years from now, I would like to come back to the earth for a few minutes just to see what the "boobs" are thinking about.

Dr. Coon's Retirement

To the Engineering Students of Georgia Tech.

Your formidable petition that I reconsider my decision to sever my relations with Ga. Tech has been received by me with feelings of profound thankfulness and pleasure. This impressive evidence of your confidence and esteem is most gratifying. I can not adequately express to you my gratitude.

I intended to leave Tech two years ago, but President Matheson refused to present my letter to the Board of Trustees, so I just had to stay!

In the ordinary course of nature I am not likely to enjoy life very much longer, and I hope, by leaving while I still have my faculties in fair repair, to do certain things I am unable to do if I remain here longer. I am sorry to disappoint those students who hoped to be in my classes. I shall not lose interest in you, and I shall hope to be on the roof during football and in my chair by the players' bench at baseball.

It goes without saying that this is not the place to preach a sermon, but I can not refrain from assuring you that I think it is a very hopeful sign that so many of our very best young men, and women too, are becoming less concerned about what lies in the future, after we have finished our work here, and are devoting their talent, their energies, to fit themselves to carry on the work of this busy and strenuous life in the most efficient way they can, to get as much out of it that is worth living, to make it more worth living not only for themselves but for their brothers, as lies in their power.

The pace that is set about you will be determined by yourselves. To you, whose knowledge and understanding are based on evidence and investigation of things in Nature about you, which is Science, instead of relying upon musty mediaevalism,—on you is the responsibility of determining the ideals of conduct and right living for those who can not think for themselves, but must be led.

Again expressing to you my heartfelt thanks for your solicitation, and a reverent longing for you to attain the highest ethical and moral success of which man is capable, I am,

> Gratefully yours,
> J. S. Coon,
> May 21, 1923.